Take
My Moments
and
My Days

Tales from the Next Step Community
Year Three

Edited by Justin Rossow

TAKE MY MOMENTS AND MY DAYS:
TALES FROM THE NEXT STEP COMMUNITY, YEAR THREE

ISBN: 9798357958471

38, 39, and 40 were originally written by Visual Faith® Coach Valerie Matyas for the 2022 Creative Haven Retreat. Used by permission.

Modified parts of 41. What Do You Need to Follow Jesus? show up in *My Next Step: A How-To Companion for People Who Want to Follow Jesus (But Sometimes Get Stuck) Volume 1: Getting Started* by Justin Rossow, Next Step Press: Ann Arbor, MI. © 2022. Used by permission.

Cover design: Brett Jordan, bit.ly/brett_blog
Cover image: unsplash.com/photos/YxqLwUeSOBs
Proofreading: Proofreading: Kay Baxter and Deanna Rossow

Inquiries or comments may be directed to: Innovation@findmynextstep.org.

We help you take a next step

Edited by
Justin Rossow

With contributions from
Alli Bauck
Kristeen A. Bruun
Conrad Gempf
Heidi Goehmann
Katie Helmreich
Rachel Hinz
Ted Hopkins
Kim Longden
Valerie Matyas
Amy Meyer
Raelyn Pracht
Justin Rossow
Naomi Rossow

Table of Contents

INTRODUCTION

How do you live out your faith in the midst of your everyday life? That simple question helped launch The Next Step Community as a place where real people actively look for what Jesus is doing in their ordinary lives, and then share an insight or encouragement along the way.

The articles in this anthology, originally published on our blog at **community.findmynextstep.org** between October 2021 and September 2022, continue to tell the *Tales from the Next Step Community* we began with *Jesus at the Center of My Messy Life* (2020) and *Be Still and Notice* (2021). You won't find simple, silver-bullet answers from these bloggers. But you will find an attitude of expectation, a playful wondering if Jesus might be up to something in our mundane habits, normal conversations, weekly work schedules, and family routines.

You'll hear from real people who are often struggling, sometimes failing, and consistently looking for where Jesus is speaking into their particular situations, how the Spirit might be shaping their response, and what promise from the Father propels their next step.

The title for this year's anthology, *Take My Moments and My Days*, is taken from an article by blogger Katie Helmreich; but, of course, Katie took that phrase from the familiar hymn, "Take My Life, and Let It Be."

That hymn is a prayer of consecration, dedicating again to the Lord's service my hands and feet; my voice and lips; my silver and gold; my intellect, will, heart, love, life, and self—all those moments and days that, put together, make up my own journey of faith in this world.

Like you, our Next Step Community bloggers are trying to live out that dependence on Jesus moment to moment, day to day. Their stories are an invitation to you to join the adventure—to try, and fail, and get up and try again—to live under an umbrella of grace that makes even your daily grind a place you can expect Jesus to show up. The Jesus to whom we dedicate our lives first dedicated himself to us: that eternal confidence covers all your moments and your days.

1. Take My Moments and My Days

By Katie Helmreich

My alarm went off at 5:50 this morning. I hit snooze a few times, but then I remembered today's the day I'd arranged to swap kid-free hours with a friend of mine!

Before coffee, head still on the pillow, my mind started racing, trying to figure out how to be the most efficient with my solo time this morning: I should brain dump the whole week's to-do list and really decide the best use of each hour. I should order groceries now so that I can pick them up when I'm out getting the kids. I wish my meeting was earlier in the morning so I'd have the answers I need to move forward with XYZ a bit sooner. Can't forget to pack lunches! Do they need swimsuits? Jackets?... On and on it went.

The storm of frantic energy got bigger and bigger. I could feel my creative brain cowering in the corner as the fear of wasting my alone time got more and more overpowering. I have this gift of a quiet house, and my drive to maximize the heck out of it was trashing all the calm, creative, joy. The need to make the most of each moment threatened to completely squash any chance of productivity.

Do you know the feeling? When time is so precious, you don't want to lose a second; and, as a result, you risk wasting it all?

As I drove home from dropping off the kids, I found myself inadvertently humming that timeless hymn, "Take My Life and Let It Be."

As my fists clenched the steering wheel, I was also clinging tightly to the mindset "my time is scarce; my time is precious." But then I realized what I was humming. "...take my moments and my days, let them flow in ceaseless praise."

The truth is, every moment before and behind me is a gift from God. My Father, who created time itself, has given me this morning. Not for my own gain or to use in a way that feeds my "got it together" ego. Not even for the end result of any project I undertake.

Every moment I'm given is a moment I get to give back to God. The Spirit guides my mind, my heart, and my hands, allowing me to glorify God in ordinary everyday ways.

The value in these moments isn't what I get done. It's who I'm here for. It's how I love others and show them Jesus.

So this morning I need to notice that I'm here for my husband, helping to manage things while he's away at work so that he doesn't have to add them to his task list. I'm here for my kids. Even though they're at a friend's house at the moment, I get to show them what it looks like to work hard, to work well, to use your gifts to bless others.

I'm here for the author of this book we're working on together. She has a dream and I get to help her see it on shelves someday! I'm here for my friend and his start-up business. I'm here for his customers, taking the stress out of producing something worthwhile, even if they couldn't quite picture it on their own.

I'm here for my friend, returning the gift of quiet time to use as she needs this afternoon. I'm here for her kids. It's a joy and an honor to be part of supporting each other's kids and showing them they're not the only ones following Jesus.

I'm here for Jesus. I'm here because of Jesus. Because He led me here to be his hands and feet. The purpose of my every moment is to glorify God and to love others.

What does that look like this morning? I'm still not quite clear on the details. But I'm no longer tempted to hoard my time. I'll take a look at that list, and see where it goes. The details will sort themselves out.

I know my purpose. The peace that brings is priceless.

"Take my love, my Lord, I pour at Thy feet its treasures store; Take myself, and I will be ever, only, all for Thee."

◆——————————————————————————◆

At Next Step Press, we like to begin our publications with *JJ*, a Latin abbreviation we borrowed from J.S. Bach. *JJ* stands for "Jesus, help!" We also like to end with Bach's *Soli Deo Gloria*: "To God alone, glory!"

In between JJ and SDG we invite you to explore the adventure of following Jesus with us. We aren't getting this exactly right all the time; but Jesus is faithful. As we commit our moments and our days to the regular habit of taking small steps following Jesus, we also commit to the practice of following Jesus with other people. When we walk together we see more than we would all on our own.

These stories are a record of Jesus at work in our ordinary lives. But their purpose is to help you see Jesus at work in your ordinary life, too. Welcome to the adventure of following Jesus!

WALKING WITH

We follow Jesus better when we follow him together. That's one of the basic premises of The Next Step Community. From small conversations with friends, to simple acts of service, to the challenge of facing cultural change, our communal faith requires community.

Walking with others on this journey of faith can give us insight into how the eternal God is at work in the regular relationships that mark our common, finite moments and all-too-ordinary days.

2. Small Conversations

By Justin Rossow

Sid is good at her job; and her job right now is to help unfreeze my frozen shoulder, something that has to be painful in order for it to work. So with a river of icepicks shooting down my arm as Sid wrenches my shoulder into another awkward position, I asked the diminutive Indian woman what she does for fun.

I know; it seems like a strange question to ask in the middle of a torture session, but I was simply taking a conversation that started around God's Word into the normal places I go every week. You see, we're practicing small conversations at my home congregation right now; nothing too heroic or too involved. We're just trying to develop the habit of keeping God's Word on our minds and in our mouths as we go about our everyday lives.

We had been talking about delight in my staff meeting right before PT, so I just kept that faith conversation going. I didn't cite chapter or verse. I didn't invite Sid to worship. I didn't even tell her where I work! I just slipped *the thing we were talking about in Bible study* into the small talk of the rest of my day.

It turns out, Sid and her fiancé like to travel for fun. And Sid also likes to cook as a form of recreation. I used to live next to some wonderful Indian women who loved to cook all kinds of curry and other Indian dishes, so I asked what she enjoys cooking most. Tacos, she said. But they have to be moist; not like the dry ones you get at restaurants. And she has a goal of making ravioli from scratch. In fact, she was signing up for an online class to learn how.

The conversation didn't go the way I expected, but I enjoyed hearing about what brings Sid joy. I even told her how cool it was that, while we started talking about *playful delight*, she immediately went to *delicious delight*—two different kinds of delight I had been reading about in a book just that morning.

Then it happened: Sid asked me the name of the book.

Now, I have been in PT at this location off and on for six months, and I don't think any of the regulars know what I do for a living. I haven't mentioned Jesus or the Bible. It just hasn't come up. But all of a sudden, this person who was just filling in for the day, this woman whom I just met (and who was in the process of what felt like removing a limb from my body) was asking me specifically about *Delight! Discipleship as the Adventure of Loving and Being Loved.*

So I told her the title and a little of what the book is about. I said religious people sometimes experience faith as a burden (that got a small grunt from Sid). I mentioned how I thought Jesus intended a relationship with Him to be full of exploration, and adventure, and curiosity, and even fun.

And you know what? Sid didn't ask to be baptized. She wasn't in church on Sunday. We just had a nice conversation, she finished tearing my arm from its socket, and we went on with our daily routines.

But something was happening inside my heart during that whole interaction. I was practicing seeing my ordinary life through the lens of the part of God's Word that had already invaded my day. And I was trying to get that word into my mouth in an ordinary conversation. I saw delight through Sid's eyes; and that helped me see Jesus more clearly, too.

You never know how or when one of those small conversations will crop up. But I don't think that faith conversation in physical therapy would have happened at all if we hadn't just been talking about it in a staff meeting at church. It takes some getting used to, but keeping your eyes peeled for God's Word in your week will make you more likely to see God's Word active in your life outside of Sunday morning.

So we're asking people to practice looking for some small way to have a faith conversation outside of our regular church meeting times and spaces. Any kind of "faith conversation" can feel daunting, especially outside of worship! I mean, what comes to mind when you try to imagine a "faith conversation"? Knocking on a stranger's door to ask if they have a saving relationship with Jesus? Handing out religious tracts at a football stadium? Traveling halfway around the world to serve the lowest and least?

While these kinds of activities can bring real benefit, the idea behind a small faith conversation in your ordinary week is much simpler. The goal of these conversations is less about reaching out to people who don't know Jesus, and more about planting God's Word deeper in our own hearts by interacting with others. (We follow Jesus better when we follow him together.)

Sometimes those simple conversations may lead to a deeper engagement, but that's not really the focus. The main idea is simply this: if we talk about what we are learning or hearing from Jesus *with other people in our everyday experience,* God's Word will become a more and more natural part of our ordinary lives. And when God's Word is a normal, regular, expected, natural, obvious part of our normal lives, some really amazing things start to happen.

You don't have to quote the Bible.

You don't have to sign anyone up for church.

You don't have to make a Gospel presentation.

Just be curious about how something you are hearing in God's Word right now will connect to the rest of your regular week. Then watch for what happens next. Sometimes *looking for something* is all it takes to see that *it was there all along.*

The weekend after I met Sid in PT, one of our Elders was eager to tell me about a small conversation he had during his ordinary work week. The Elders had just been talking about looking for those faith conversations wherever they crop up, so he was ready to lean in when one unexpectedly came his way.

Heading into his work building, he ran into a coworker; a fellow Christian in a rather secular environment. "How are you doing?" our Elder was asked. His response was something less than delightful. But when he asked the same question in return, his coworker replied: "I'm great! My family loves me, my faith is strong, and I am gainfully employed!"

Or something like that; I have forgotten the exact details. The point is, my friend the Elder was excited to tell me about this almost throw-away conversation *because it made him immediately recognize God's Word in a common, ordinary setting.*

So right there in the entryway he took a small next step to engage. He said to his coworker, "You know what? How about we pray together before we go into work?"

And they did.

No mountains moved.

No voice came from heaven.

Nothing spectacular or miraculous took place; just two guys, heading into their ordinary day job, with schedules filled to overflowing, taking time to say a quick prayer before getting back to the grind.

(On second thought, maybe that is rather miraculous...)

So we're practicing small conversations at my home congregation right now. I'd invite you to run that experiment, too. You don't have to do anything too heroic or too involved. Just begin to develop the habit of keeping God's Word on your mind and in your mouth as you go about your everyday life.

Take a word or phrase from your weekly worship or from your time in God's Word and carry it out into the rest of your week. Ask a question, any question, of a neighbor or friend. Be curious about the people around you. And be on the lookout for ways in which God's Word shows up in common, ordinary places.

My guess is, as we train ourselves to connect God's Word to our small conversations with other people in our regular routine, we'll gain a deeper appreciation of what Jesus is up to in our lives; certainly in Sunday worship, but during all the other hours of our week, too.

3. Ivy for Dana

By Kristeen Bruun

I attend a lot of funerals. Partly, as I age, I of course know more people who die. But also, I grew up in a small town at a time when everyone sent casseroles and went to funerals, and I've never given up the practice.

I was surprised when a friend once gave as his reason for not attending a funeral: "I just don't like funerals." Well, who does? I thought. But the woman who had died was the mother of a friend, so I wanted to stand by his side. Sometimes that's all you can do—just show up. "Weep with those who weep," St. Paul says (Romans 12:15b). Sometimes the funerals do make me weep, as I recall the many friends and family that I have sent on ahead.

The flowers that accompany funerals make me think of the garden out of which we were formed (Genesis 2:8-9). After the Lord God formed human beings of dust from the ground, God then planted a garden in Eden. So we surround our beloved dead with the symbols of life that recall our origins. It doesn't matter whether or not the people who participate in this horticultural ritual can articulate the underlying reason for it; the flowers speak for themselves.

My co-worker Dana's brother just died of Covid a couple of weeks ago. Phillip was younger than Dana by five years. During the time between his death and the funeral, I got to listen as Dana told the stories of their growing up together; some of them funny, and some of them touching. "I helped raise him," Dana said over and over.

Covid delayed the funeral for a bit. Did she need food? No, they had everything they needed. How about flowers? Not really—there would be plenty. But what Dana really wanted was ivy. She had ivy from her mother's grave, and ivy from her father's grave, and she had managed to keep the plants growing for ten or twelve years.

Phillip was going to be cremated, so he would not have a grave, but Dana still wanted ivy. "If you want ivy, you should have ivy," I told her. Then I started looking for ivy…

I went first to my usual online floral source. No ivy. It possibly would have helped if I had known a little more about what I was looking for, but all I know about ivy is: the roots go in the ground, the green stuff should be on top, and DON'T OVERWATER IT. I went on to check out a couple of local flower vendors. I guess ivy is not very popular. No ivy.

The day of the funeral came and went. I sat and prayed, wept with the other mourners, and went away tired and somewhat frustrated.

Coming into church the next day for Sunday worship, I saw a fellow congregant whom I knew ran a garden center in a local small town. I hadn't thought of Michele before because her center was forty miles away. As soon as I said ivy, Michele began to tell me all the different kinds and varieties and subspecies she stocks. "Stop," I told her. "Just pick out something that won't die."

So she did; and she worked out a way to have it delivered through a mutual friend. When I came into work on Tuesday morning I was met by a lush green plant sitting in my chair with leaves cascading over the sides of the pot. I called Dana back to my office and watched her smile through her tears. "It's perfect," she said. "Just what I was hoping for."

Life began in a garden. According to the book of Revelation, it will end there as well. On either side of the river of the water of life grows the Tree of Life, and "the leaves of the tree were for the healing of the nations" (Revelation 22:1-2).

Perfect healing awaits the End of Days, but the earthly gifts of God can soothe our souls already now. Like ivy, lush and green; and a reminder of God's garden.

4. Go and Tell a Friend about Jesus

By Kim Longden

I've noticed that lessons for children in Bible curriculums oftentimes end with an exhortation for them to go and tell a friend about Jesus. This puts an image in my head of a five-year-old laying out an apologetic Gospel presentation to a friend, and makes me chuckle at the thought. When would that ever even happen? Ha!

But that thought, in turn, puts a picture in my head of me laying out said apologetic Gospel presentation to one of my friends ... and humbly wondering, *when has that ever happened*? What started as a simple charge at the end of a children's lesson becomes an overwhelming thought of how and when to "go and tell a friend about Jesus"—not only for the kids, but for me as well.

As I've pondered "telling a friend about Jesus" over the years, I've realized that maybe my vision of an apologetic Gospel presentation isn't necessarily what these kids' Bible lessons are referring to. I've noticed that we "tell about Jesus" in every day conversations in many different ways; maybe there is a more realistic place to start that doesn't seem as overwhelming as my imaginary five-year-old theology professor.

So how does Jesus start showing up more often in our everyday conversations? Just like with many things, I think a good place to start is by practicing at home. The more we talk about the Gospel—good news!—of Jesus in our homes with those closest to us, the more Jesus becomes a natural part of our thoughts and speech patterns in areas of life outside of the home, as well.

One easy place to start is noticing and talking about God's goodness in nature. When opening the blinds in the morning and the glorious sun streams in, we say, "What a beautiful day God has given us!" Or when an anticipated heavy rainstorm breaks forth finally after a dry spell, we thank God for this gift that only the Almighty can provide—sometimes we even give thanks by running out into the downpour and enjoying it! We commend God's artistry on a beautiful sunset, or marvel out loud at the Creative Majesty while gazing at the stars. Nature already stirs in our hearts praise for our Creator, and practicing praising God out loud at home with our families helps doing so become more natural when we're around others.

Another way to practice "telling about Jesus" is sharing stories with each other of when we've seen God's presence in our lives. Big or small, we can be on the lookout for ways God is working and share them around the dinner table or driving in the car.

I'm reminded of a time when my young son accidentally got too close to a bird's nest. The young birds inside were close to fledging, but hadn't left the nest yet. His presence startled them, and they all haphazardly flew out of the nest with squawking and commotion while the momma bird tried to round them back up. We watched the scene helplessly and felt terrible because we knew the mom wouldn't be able to get the babies back in the nest and there was nothing we could do to help.

It was evening, so we prayed that the babies would be safe overnight and that their wings would strengthen enough to be able to fly so they would not be so vulnerable. The next morning when we looked out, we saw the mom with her little babies all huddled by our deck like they were waiting for something. As soon as we saw them, the momma started hopping around in the grass looking for food and the babies flew up into low branches of the pine tree.

We started laughing and clapping! The fledglings had made it through the night and could fly a little higher! Our prayer had been answered! God not only answered our prayer, but gave my son, who felt terrible, the gift of knowing that the babies were OK. We thanked God for this grace, and we retell this story often around our dinner table.

These are the stories about Jesus I could envision a little child sharing with a friend more than that well-laid-out Gospel presentation, because this IS good news to a little child! That big God we talk about at church is also a God who cares about me personally. Jesus cares about me enough to show my young son that the baby birdies were OK. Telling these stories over and over at home weaves them into our lives, and makes it more natural to share them with others as God provides opportunities.

As adults we can also practice noticing and then sharing stories at home of the good news of Jesus working in the details of our lives. I'm reminded of another time when we had unexpected company for lunch and, at the first glance of my cupboards, my situation seemed much like Old Mother Hubbard's. While I was contemplating what we'd eat, I remembered that a church friend had just given us some delicious bakery bread and I was able to pull together a pretty hearty cold cut sandwich lunch. Like with the loaves and fishes, we had plenty to eat!

My kids are used to me saying *"That's how God do!"* in moments like this when I realize that details were already being worked out before I even knew that a need was going to exist. When we see that God has miraculously provided for a need—big or small—or when Jesus brings us comfort in a trying situation, we can share this with each other in the home; which makes sharing it become more natural in our conversations outside of the home, too.

Talking about these things at home not only encourages us as a family, but it puts these stories on the forefront of our thoughts so that they're on our lips when we're interacting with people out and about. Maybe the entry way to a fuller Gospel presentation is not a five-year-old with a theological PowerPoint presentation. Maybe telling a friend about Jesus doesn't mean reciting the Nicene Creed or covering the Treatise on the Power and Primacy of the Pope.

Maybe, just maybe, what my kids and my neighbor and the guy down the street all need to hear first is that *Jesus is active and present in the details in my life*, and He *cares about the details in their lives, too*. Maybe that's what it means to "go and tell a friend about Jesus."

5. Our Next (Hard) Project

By Katie Helmreich

Ben and I are project people. We've been building things together since our early dating days (some twenty years ago) and haven't really stopped since! Our next project is a big one by necessity. And we're already exhausted. Too overwhelmed and too busy to start...

We love projects! We have the necessary experience. We're all longing to use the updated space. So why can't we get this one off the ground?

Projects are hard. The memories of the long hours, stress, disagreements, aching backs, and parenting from the top of a ladder are poignant...

Sometimes the next step is familiar. *Too* familiar.

We're not afraid we're taking a step into the unknown; instead, we aren't sure we're up for going through *that* again.

So Jesus, in His perfect wisdom, blessed us with a side project. A bit of a scenic overlook. A little jog off the main trail, as the Holy Spirit encouraged us to get our bearings and recall the many ways the Father provides.

A Christian camp near us needed help with some renovations before summer programming begins. The way we got involved is so random it can only have been a God thing. But suddenly we were all in: taking pictures of the project needs, making plans, writing lists, filling shopping carts, inviting others to join us, and packing for a work weekend!

We had big goals for such a short amount of time, but we accomplished all the things we set out to do while we were there this past weekend. We even had time for a couple extra side projects!

I was really struck by how quickly I forgot what things at the camp looked like at the beginning of our weekend. It was only two days earlier, but when you're working and staying focused on what's next, it's easy to lose track of just how far you've come, and how you got there!

If my memory of how far we'd come in a two day camp project is sketchy, chances are good my memories of our past family project experiences are even less complete.

For example, the first thing that comes to mind when I think back to our major house rebuild? *"I was never more exhausted. Never more stressed. Never more out of my depth. Never hit rock bottom like I did near the end of that project..."*

Hang on! How is *that* the headline?!

If my memory of the steps we took *back then* is affecting my ability to take our next steps *now*, then it's time to revisit.

If I page through those memories in more detail, I recall laughter and bonding experiences with all who helped us! I remember the exhilaration of turning on the lights for the first time. I notice how many new skills we picked up during that year. I appreciate all over again the advice of experts during that time. I remember the encouragement from unexpected places. I can see the incredible foundation of support we had from our family. I marvel at God's steadfast love and faithful provision throughout!

Even more incredible? The deeply challenging circumstances of our most difficult projects gradually equipped us for service in ways we'd never have been able to undertake before!

Sure, projects are hard. But the Holy Spirit transforms us in those moments. If a can of paint can have a magical effect on a dingy bathroom, how much more miraculous is the way our Wonderful Counselor grants us endurance, character, and hope as we seek to "keep in step with the Spirit" (Gal. 5:25)?

The memories of hardship are easy to hold onto. But with a little effort, the memories of God's faithfulness in every circumstance come flooding back. When we recall how Jesus has kept His promise to sustain us and to equip us for service in the Kingdom, it's easier to face the next step.

Sometimes the next step is familiar. *Too* familiar.

But God was with us then; God's steadfast love got us through the last time. Jesus is with us now; He'll be with us every step of the way!

Our family and friends are with us, too. This past weekend wouldn't have been possible without them! Serving alongside them was a precious gift and a vivid reminder of the many times we've been able to help one another.

Familiar next steps can be tough; but, as always, they're easier when we take them together!

Ben and I will tackle this next renovation soon. Not because we're all sunshine and optimism about how fun it will be, but because it needs to be done. We can do hard things, even when we realize going into them just how much it will take.

Growth isn't easy. But, as I learned again this weekend working at that camp, the opportunity to see how far we've come is amazing!

This morning I'm still sore from sanding drywall on the ceiling of a bunkhouse, so I was surprised to find that I think of our work weekend as a "scenic overlook." But maybe it's fitting: the best views are often at the top of challenging trails!

It is a blessing to look back over our family projects and marvel at all God has done to prepare us for service in the Kingdom: we would never have been able to serve at that camp without all the skills we learned with others as we worked together on our own family projects.

But what really excites me is seeing how much more there is to discover. Sure, projects are hard. And your next step may be all too familiar. But how many more opportunities will we have to serve because of the ways we are growing now? What a gift to know that the Holy Spirit transforms us in those moments!

6. I Long to See You Face to Face

By Justin Rossow

It's been a rather confusing year for worship.
We're called to stay focused on relationship.

As COVID-19 drags on (and on, and on, and on...), our novel worship experience raises a new kind of question about how we should think, feel, and act toward fellow believers in the Church. **Until recently, we only ever had two categories for church attendance:** (1) people who came, and (2) people who didn't. Over the last few decades, the category of "regular attendance" has shifted from 4+ times a month to about once a month, but the fundamental distinction between "people who go to my church" and "people who don't" was still intact. Until recently...

Now we have brand new categories like "people who only attend online;" or "people who attend my church and a bunch of other churches online;" or "people who attend regularly online, and come once in a while to in-person worship." The list goes on and on...

We could simply rejoice over the fact that online worship has actually increased worship attendance overall. But some of the feelings and thoughts we used to have about people who stopped coming to worship seem to apply fairly directly to people who still *only* (or *mostly*) attend online.

In other words, we want people to come back to church. And by that we mean, we want people to come back to *in-person* worship. So what are we supposed to think and feel about people who worship with us, but only or mostly virtually?

Personally, I have a rather mixed set of emotions about online-only worshippers. For me and my family, the sudden rise in online options precipitated by COVID-19 came at just the right moment. For the first time in our history as a family we didn't have a church home, and when COVID hit, we still didn't know where we were going to land next. Online options allowed us to worship at multiple congregations across the country and feel connected to the Church even when we didn't have a home congregation. I also found it kind of nice to worship with my family from our living room, discuss the sermon and the service together, and then seamlessly transition to brunch.

Now, a couple of years later, I still value the option and ease of online worship, even though I have a home congregation I attend weekly. Online worship gives my busy family options, and therefore allows us to make decisions to stay engaged. On a recent Sunday morning, I attended in-person worship at one location while one of my daughters attended in-person worship at a different congregation (in a different city) and my wife and two of our kids worshiped online before they headed out for a busy afternoon. **I value in-person worship. But I kind of like online worship, too.**

Not everybody feels that way. Already back in January I started getting requests to write something that would motivate people who were only worshipping online to get back to in-person worship. **I have seen pastors as well as lay people share frustration on social media about people not coming back to church.** As we get closer to another Advent/Christmas cycle, the heat behind that feeling seems to be rising.

From what I have seen, the push to get people back to in-person worship has intensified. The feeling of frustration has even boiled over in some instances to questioning the spiritual status of these online attenders. **More and more, people are thinking and feeling about online-only the way we used to think and feel about delinquent members:** they aren't here; they aren't part of us; they are probably lazy; their faith is in danger; we love them and want to win them back (or at least take them off our membership rolls).

Even if that characterization can be unkind at times, I get the perspective. People who are not with us face to face don't feel like they are part of us the same way everybody else in the room seems to be. Some aspects of our life together certainly don't translate as well (or at all) to a virtual gathering. Some people who worship online only may well be lazy (sometimes I worship online just because it's easier). And some of them probably are falling away from faith to some extent, or at least falling away from our local community of believers.

On the other hand, I know that some people see online worship not as mere convenience, but as a life line. For health or scheduling reasons, **online worship offers a real connection that would otherwise be all but impossible.** At the very least, **virtual services offer people an option** between the absolutes of either skipping worship or being at a specific location at a specific time. Online options sometimes make worship possible in ways face to face worship does not and can not.

Even if the reasons for virtual attendance sometimes seem like excuses, I understand the perspective of people who prefer to worship remotely. With hectic schedules and divided opinions about masking and vaccinating, online can feel like a safe option that not only makes worship convenient, but *possible*.

So how are we supposed to think and feel about people across the spectrum on the virtual vs face to face worship continuum? I think the Apostle Paul, in his very low-tech communication environment, might have some help for us.

Paul's first letter to the church at Thessalonica is a study in long-distance relationships. In chapter 3, Paul makes this comment:

> We pray most earnestly night and day that we may see you
> face to face and supply what is lacking in your faith.

1 Thessalonians 3:10 (ESV)

Paul seems to think the Thessalonians are missing something, something they can only get face to face, in person. Without further context, Paul's words could seem like clear biblical support for an "online worship isn't *really* worship" perspective, or at least for a "you are missing something important if you aren't here in person" approach. In fact, without further context, you might assume Paul is concerned about the faithfulness or even the faith of these Thessalonians, lacking as it is in something essential that can only be delivered face to face.

Read around in 1 Thessalonians a little bit more, however, and a very different picture emerges. At one time, Paul was indeed concerned about their faith—but with the recent report from Timothy, Paul is almost giddy with love and affection for these people he dearly misses.

Paul uses all kinds of relational images to describe his long-distance relationship to the Thessalonians. Paul can describe his own ministry among them as a "**nursing mother** taking care of her own children" (2:7) and "like **a father** with his children" (2:11). Paul is both father and mother to these faithful believers, and they are at the same time like his parents, for losing a face to face relationship with the Thessalonians was dramatic and traumatic from Paul's perspective: "when we were **orphaned** by being separated from you for a short time (in person, not in thought), out of our intense longing we made every effort to see you" (2:17).

Paul says their ongoing separation was caused by Satan himself, but that obstacle to their relationship could not hinder familial love and longing. Paul's abundant joy in hearing of the Thessalonians and their faithfulness and ongoing relationship brings rich praise to God and a renewed longing to see them in real time, face to face.

From everything Paul says in his letter, it's clear that the Thessalonians aren't lacking something when it comes to trust or salvation. In fact, Paul celebrates their faith! So what is the thing "lacking" in their faith that Paul thinks he can only remedy by an in-person visit?

In context, I suspect **the thing they are lacking that can only be remedied face to face is** *being together with Paul face to face*. The one thing you can only get in person is *being together in person*. And being in the same room would be valuable both for Paul and for the Thessalonians, so much so that Paul prays, longs, and plans for that face to face visit, even though he already knows his friends are standing firm in the faith.

In the meantime, **Paul uses all of the resources and technology at his disposal to maintain a relationship with these people he dearly loves, even though he cannot see them face to face right now.**

- Paul sends Timothy to them in person, as a virtual Paul, to spend some face time with the Thessalonian church and share encouragement with them and from them.
- Paul prays earnestly and repeatedly for these people he can't see right now, and invites their prayers.
- Paul uses the most current communication practices—*writing a letter and having it read to everyone in the group*—as a means of expressing relationship and passing on encouragement for faith and practice.

Paul does everything he can to stay connected to the Thessalonians while at the same time longing for that part of a mutual relationship that happens uniquely face to face.

Here may be a way forward for all of us wondering how to think and feel about online worship attendance. On the one hand, we recognize and long for the unique benefits of being face to face. On the other hand, we do absolutely everything we can to uphold and maintain the relationship, even during a time of separation. And above all, the love and longing and encouragement we share in Jesus drives us to pray for each other, and to pray for the time when we get to share faith in person again.

So if you have been frustrated by the people who have been slow to come back to regular, in-person worship, take a cue from Paul and **find ways to express your love and longing for them as valued individuals** more than you express frustration at their absence. Satan does want to divide us, and that includes dividing our hearts from each other as well as making face to face discipleship more difficult than ever. Use every communication tool at your disposal, including online worship, to maintain and encourage a faith relationship of mutual respect and trust. Pray for the people you miss seeing in worship.

And if you are still avoiding regular, in-person worship, take a cue from Paul and **find ways to express your love and longing for your community**, especially for people who may sometimes wonder if your faith is still strong and if you still love them like you used to. Paul's joy at hearing Timothy's report about the Thessalonians reminds us that **we need to communicate relationship even more clearly when we are apart for a time.**

If you aren't attending in-person worship right now for whatever reason, look for ways you can still follow Jesus in some kind of face to face relationship, with even just one or two other people. We follow Jesus better when we follow him together, and Paul seems to think some aspects of our faith can only be supplied face to face. Then pray for the people in your faith community, even when you aren't in person on Sunday morning.

Looking toward the future, I don't see us getting less busy any time soon, so weekend schedules aren't going to suddenly become more free. The threat of the next variant or the next pandemic means that, at any time, meeting virtually could suddenly become a necessity again. Seeing businesses and schools find new ways of making online work for them, I imagine **some kind of online options will become all but necessary for congregations to meet people where they live, as people live more and more online.**

The current mix of emotions and practices we are experiencing with virtual worship right now is a dress rehearsal for the new norm of online and face to face existing side by side in community. Whether that scares you or excites you, you'll want to move into that new reality with Paul's letter to his beloved Thessalonians ringing in your ears.

Can we imagine a mix of people who worship in a variety of ways, some almost always in person, some almost always virtually, and some who find themselves fluctuating between online and face to face–who all still love each other and belong to each other?

Can we imagine those people continuing to express love and longing for each other, whether together virtually or in person? Can we imagine mutual prayers, and clear communication that expresses *longing* more than frustration, *unity* over division, common *faith* over fear, and *love* over all else?

How might we take note of the schemes of the devil to divide and separate us, and then find the trust in Jesus that makes those schemes seem weak and futile? How might we maintain connection and relationship even as we muddle through the confusion of how and when and where to be together face to face?

Those questions go beyond getting people to come back to in-person worship. They speak to **what kind of community we are going to be as we grow into a new communications environment.** Will we get it right? Certainly not! Or at least, not right away.

But already now we get to play in the swirling currents of *online* and *in-person* learning, and formation, and worship, and faith in confidence that, even though we only see as through a glass, darkly, the time will come when we will see face to face.

Come quickly, Lord!

7. EMMA

By Kristeen Bruun

Ever since Emma turned twelve (she'll be fourteen in a month) and could therefore fly without paying an extra surcharge for being an unaccompanied minor, she has every so often come to visit me. We have always had great times together. We have gotten manicures, gone to a painting workshop, and always hit the used bookstore.

Emma and her family do not belong to a church, so church attendance is a mystery to her. Because this is a difficult topic with my son, I have been very careful not to push my beloved religion on Emma.

However, when she first started her visits, she had to come to church with me because I was teaching Sunday school. I was grateful that she didn't seem to mind. The last time she came, I had transitioned out of teaching. I assumed that church would not be her choice because it wasn't part of her normal world. But it was Emma who brought it up, "Are we going to church and Sunday school?"

"I'm not teaching anymore," I said. "We don't have to go."

"But I want to go," Emma said. Then I asked her if she wanted to attend adult Sunday school with me or go to the youth class. She chose the youth class and very independently trotted off.

When we met up in church, I asked the Director of Christian Education how the class had gone. "Fine," was her answer. Emma participated well and clearly enjoyed being there.

At a recent family gathering, I overheard Emma telling someone, "The people at my grandma's church like me. They remember who I am and some of them even remember my name."

I'm not sure where this is going (either this blog, or my church community's relationship with Emma). The simple acts of human recognition and hospitality are so easy to dismiss as inconsequential, even by someone with a long history of church activity such as myself. Yet clearly, they speak to the open heart.

Emma is not yet talking God-talk. But she is eager to return to Trinity. Even if she never was able to come to Trinity again, she would approach her next church experience with a positive outlook.

I want to remember her experience.

I want to smile more, reach out more, give without expectation of return. This is what my fellow congregants did with Emma. They have no way of knowing about her response. I think they would say that these little gestures don't matter much.

But, of course, they do.

I haven't said the name of Jesus yet, because he hasn't been part of the story. Except that he really has been. People who were following Jesus touched the heart of a little girl by simple acts of kindness.

> Therefore welcome one another as Christ has welcomed you,
> for the glory of God.
>
> *Romans 15:7 (ESV)*

8. A Ripple Effect of Blessings

By Amy Meyer

I was pleasantly surprised by what God did with me during and after my experience being a guest on the Next Step Podcast. I was asked to be a guest along with Pat Maier on the *Light in the Darkness* series discussing the hymn "Infant Holy, Infant Lowly." It was a lot of fun to discover the similarities that Pat and I have in our love for journaling and being intentional about praying for our neighbors.

We recorded the episode on a Tuesday afternoon, and two days later I would drive to Tennessee to be with my mom and visit my dad in the hospital. I had printed off the hymn and the coloring sheet and tucked them in my journal not knowing how God would use them to be a blessing to me again and again.

When we were visiting Dad in the hospital, he was not able to finish his thoughts or carry on much of a conversation. My mom and I both like to sing, and so we started singing familiar Christmas carols for Dad. We went through quite a few different ones, and then I pulled out the lyrics to Infant Holy, Infant Lowly and sang that one for him.

A wave of peace washed over me as I looked into my dad's eyes and sang, **"Thus rejoicing, free from sorrow, praises voicing, greet the morrow: Christ the Babe was born for you! Christ the Babe was born for you!"**

I found myself repeating those lyrics over and over as I drove back home. Over the next couple of weeks, I put it at the bottom of emails I sent to people before Christmas: "Christ the Babe was born for you." Those words reminded me just how personal and intimate the gift of Jesus is for each of us.

Then I received an email from Justin Rossow from Next Step Press with a copy of the final podcast so I could listen and share it. As I read the notes about Pat included in our episode, I saw the website for Visual Faith™ Ministry. I knew about this ministry but had never been on their website before, so I took a look.

The next thing I knew I was listening to the recorded Bible study from March of 2021 about Abiding. They were taking a look at Psalm 91, the very part of Scripture that I was looking at earlier in the day.

Whoever dwells in the shelter of the Most High
    will rest in the shadow of the Almighty.
I will say of the Lord, "He is my refuge and my fortress,
    my God, in whom I trust."
Surely he will save you
    from the fowler's snare
    and from the deadly pestilence.
He will cover you with his feathers,
    and under his wings you will find refuge;
    his faithfulness will be your shield and rampart.
You will not fear the terror of night,
    nor the arrow that flies by day,
nor the pestilence that stalks in the darkness,
    nor the plague that destroys at midday.

Psalm 91:1-6 (NIV)

God knew that I needed to hear those words again and soak in that promise a little longer. I was reminded of the beautiful image of nestling under the wings of God in a safe and warm place, like a mother hen with her chicks. And I smiled at how God uses different people in different places to bring His message to the world.

It reminded me that God is always working: sometimes we don't see it, and sometimes it is very obvious.

Regardless if we see it or we don't, Jesus is working. Jesus sees you. He hears you. Jesus is with you. And He loves you.

I am grateful that I was asked to be on a podcast, and for the ripple effect of blessings that came from saying yes. What a delightful surprise.

Amy Meyer is cofounder of Neighboring Life, an online community launched in 2022 to help us imagine neighborhoods where every person belongs, where every person knows they matter, and everyone has a contribution to make, a story to share.

9. Change? Who Said Anything about Change?

By Ted Hopkins

Almost every Lutheran knows the old joke about how many Lutherans it takes to change a light bulb. "Change? Who said anything about change?" After an initial chortle, this joke always hits pretty close to home for me. Change is hard. More than that, I don't like change. I'm only willing to accept change when I'm deeply unhappy. And even then, I would rather have other people change to make life better for me.

Change takes will and effort, and it's often awkward. I don't want to deal with that. I am pretty comfortable with everyone accommodating me—see how flexible I am!—but I don't want to change myself.

I think many Christians feel the same way about our own congregations. When I started dating my wife, Beth, I found out that Baptists have the same joke Lutherans do, but with a minor variation: "How many *Baptists* does it take to change a light bulb?" Across denominations, we tend to sit in the same pew, hang out with the same friends, and feel comforted by the same sermon style week after week. Change? Who said anything about change?

The ancient Greek philosopher Heraclitus once claimed that a person can never go through the same river twice. The point was not only that the water was changing—an obvious point about currents—but that a person is constantly fluctuating, too. The next time she enters the river, her experiences will be different, her relationships will be different, and even her cells will be different. Everything changes.

This ever-changing, topsy-turvy reality ought to feel familiar to us. At least, it feels familiar to me. Let me give you an example. Not too long ago, I happily observed to Beth how great life was going. (This would be called *foreshadowing* if I were living in a movie...) The children were building solid friendships and getting along so well, and they were even opening up to us about important stuff. Work was going great for both of us, and we seemed to be building on meaningful friendships, established as adults even.

But within two weeks, nothing felt the same. The kids were at each other's throats. Instead of being in sync, Beth and I began to butt heads at almost everything, once even literally. (This would be called *irony*.) Work trouble started, too, and those burgeoning friendships didn't seem quite as stable as they just had.

Isn't this how life always is? Wait a few weeks, and nothing is the same...

This world of flux affects not only our personal lives, it impacts our churches, too. Over the last century, Christianity has experienced a pretty serious change in relationship to North American culture. The Christian faith does not have the same cultural capital it once did. Our religion does not have pride of place in schools, government, or even in the public sphere. Not that long ago, Christianity held all of these privileges, and others always adapted to us. But things have changed.

So, what are we going to do about all this change?

We could dig in our heels and refuse to adjust. We could act like nothing has changed. We could just keep trying to vote in politicians who will bring back the privileges we want, trying to make everyone change to fit us.

All of those options have a kind of logic that can be appealing. And all of them can be framed in pious language about theology, the Church, or Jesus. It sounds right to say that we want to "remain faithful" to Jesus. It feels holy to say that we want to "stay true" to our tradition and our faith. But all too often those religious phrases can become ways we cloak (even to ourselves) our own intransigence and discomfort with change. So, what are we going to do about all this change?

Maybe the first thing that needs to change is the question. Instead of focusing on what we are going to do, we can think first about the Word and work of God: What commands and promises does God the Father give to us for the Church in this time? How is the Spirit leading us to be formed into Jesus for this changed and changing world? How does Jesus' own life and ministry change how we relate to this new time and space?

To be clear, the Church must *not* become the culture, or even become *like* the culture. Instead, we must be faithful witnesses *to the world*, witnesses of Jesus Christ and his death and resurrection for us and *for the world*.

Faithfulness to Jesus does not permit us to avoid change.

In fact, I think it's the opposite: faithfulness to Jesus leads us to faithful change. But let's talk about that next time. (This one would be called a *cliffhanger*.)

10. Faithful Change

By Ted Hopkins

In my last post, I ended by saying faithfulness to Jesus leads us to faithful change, despite our deep and abiding reluctance to do so. In that vein, let me offer a bold thesis: the Christian life is one of continual change. **Following Jesus, by definition, means change.**

I can almost hear the naysayers: *"At the heart of Christianity is a God who doesn't change (Mal. 3:6) and a faith in God that is steadfast and immovable (1 Cor. 15:58). If Jesus is the same yesterday, and today, and forever (Heb. 13:8), and our faith is rooted in him, without wavering, how can you say that the Christian life is one of continual change?"*

To be clear, our friendly naysayers are right, both about our God and about the faith that grasps God's promises. The Word of the Lord remains forever (Is. 40:8, Mt. 24:35), and saving faith hears and believes that steadfast promise and so receives exactly what the promise says (Rom. 10:10, 17): forgiveness of sins, life, and salvation as Jesus abides in his people by faith, and we abide in him.

While the Christian life is marked by firm faith in a permanent promise, following Jesus is at the same time also marked by continual battle against the sinful flesh, by discipline and self-restraint, by pilgrimage, imitation, and adventure.

The author of Hebrews describes a life of faith as **a kind of race**, and calls us to run that race with perseverance, throwing off the sin that entangles (Heb. 12:1). In 1 Corinthians, Paul uses similar imagery to call God's people to **run with purpose** and follow God's will and direction, rather than the ways of the world. Paul even compares the life of the Christian to **a boxing match** in order to emphasize the need for discipline in our lives as we train our bodies to be ready for the fight (1 Cor. 9:24-27). In Romans, Paul describes a war going on inside of him, between what he wants to do and what he keeps on doing, a war between the sinful flesh and the Spirit of God where **you and I are the battleground** (Rom. 7:13-24).

What are these images and examples illustrating except incessant change, hearing the Word and turning to God in faith to do the Father's will rather than the will of sin that entangles our steps and deforms our desires? **The Christian life is neither pure journey nor pure destination; it is more like a relationship with another person, growing, deepening, abiding, but never remaining the same.**

At least, this is how I have experienced my relationship with my wife. Perhaps those who got married in their thirties have had to experience less change, but Beth and I were married at twenty-two.

Frankly, we didn't know what we were getting ourselves into! At that time in my life I still played a lot of videogames, and hadn't even held a full-time job yet—and wouldn't for two more years (if I'm being generous to myself).

Beth had never shared a room with someone else, let alone a boy. When we were only twenty-two, how could I imagine the person she would eventually become? How could she know the theology nerd into which I would grow?

My point is that my wife and I have changed immensely over time, and our relationship has changed along with us.

I am simply not the same man I was fifteen years ago, nor she the same woman. Our relationship has changed. But we are still married; that hasn't changed.

In fact, the truth of promises we made to each other are even more apparent now than they were back then. Our commitment to one another—to put one another first, to listen to each other, to communicate our affection, to spend time together—these things are stable foundations around which our relationship has grown.

In other words, **our promise of commitment to each other has provided a permanent platform around which we have changed.** Although we often fall short in our relationship, we have pledged to not stop being loyal to each other, working on building a life together, and putting each other first.

These "givens" provide stability in our marriage relationship; but they also require change. To live in these promises means for me to reevaluate my relationship with my wife regularly in order to be a good, faithful husband.

This stability that requires change also applies to our lives of faith. We have an unchanging Lord who is our stable foundation, whose promises are permanent, whose forgiveness is forever, and whose love is lasting; that's a given. But these promises are not ones we just receive and leave: they are promises into which we live and around which we orient our entire selves.

We must change if we are to look continually to Jesus and live in his Word. After all, the race of life is not a smooth track. We experience not only speed bumps, but steep cliffs; not just streams, but deep ravines. We face deserts—the wildernesses where God seems absent—and stormy seas—where death and the devil seem more powerful than anything else.

When the terrain gets tough, we need to change, to hear Christ's Word in our current context as forgiving our sins and comforting our afflictions, to know our present neighbors as fellow bearers of God's image, and to reevaluate how we are following Jesus according to God's Word.

The unchanging, permanent promise does not prevent change. Rather, **God's unchanging, permanent promise enables us to change**, as we daily grasp anew God's Word, and as the Spirit works in us to conform us (shape, form, mold, and change us) to the image of Jesus.

In church, we usually use the word "repentance" to refer to this kind of change. Repentance means that we turn our eyes to Jesus when we are so prone to look elsewhere—especially inward at ourselves. Repentance means turning to the Word to do what God says when we have been listening to what our ears want to hear.

Repentance means trusting in the promises of forgiveness that the loving Father offers for Jesus' sake when we have loved other things first.

And in every walk of life—from childhood to gray hair—in every relationship, and daily, we are called to repent, turn and return to Jesus, remembering his grace and mercy in every trouble, keeping our sinfulness in check in every temptation, and following him to serve every neighbor that comes into our sphere.

Hence, Luther wrote, the Lord Jesus willed "the whole life of believers to be one of repentance." In other words, **the whole life of believers (those who trust God's unswerving promises) is one of *change*.**

Such a life that orients itself to Jesus constantly, that looks to his word, to his story, and to his commands, is not a static memorial set in stone, but a beautiful and interactive adventure. This adventure is listening, looking, and living, all oriented to Jesus Christ.

Such an adventure requires change, but *faithful change* that stays rooted in Jesus.

The Word at Work

Where do you see the Word of God showing up in your life? The Word is present and active in the sermon you heard on Sunday, in the Bible class you attend regularly, in your own personal reading of Scripture, and in the conversations you've already had this week with family or friends, people like you who are trying to follow Jesus.

A careful reading of the biblical text is necessary for sustained faith; and the Word sustains your faith in a variety of ways. As the Spirit empowers your hearing and reading, you'll find real help right where you need it: eternal truths that matter for your Tuesday afternoon.

11. Great (and Not-So-Great) Expectations

By Ted Hopkins

Expectations are a funny beast. On vacation this summer, we ate at a restaurant that was a bit sketchy when we first walked in. They had open tables and could serve our large, very hungry group so we went with it, but first impressions were not positive. The décor and furniture harkened back to the late 90s, and the ambiance was more dive bar than wine bar—no offense if that's your vibe.

Few of us felt great about this choice, but we (and the children with us) were famished. With Mariana-Trench-level expectations, I was nearly astonished when the first appetizers appeared. The spinach-artichoke dip hit all the right notes, served with fresh, delicious pita. My crab cakes—don't ask me why I chose crab cakes in a place like that; in retrospect it seems ridiculous, but I have trouble saying no to a crab cake—were texturally delightful and included a lovely aioli sauce. The experience was simply enjoyable.

Contrast that with a great restaurant we also went to on the same trip. Many of us had been there before so we knew to expect perfectly cooked woodfire pizzas, cheese curds with that precise ratio of fried breading and gooey goodness, and sandwiches that surprised you with all the flavors. I was so pumped for this place; and then it fell rather flat for me. The crust of the pizza was a little overdone, and lacked the acid necessary to make the flavors pop. The cheese curds didn't quite hit home, either. Everything was fine—probably even good—but it didn't meet my own personal expectations.

The strange thing is that, while the first place was a better experience because it exceeded expectations, if I actually compare the food and the ambiance head to head, the second place still comes out on top.

The woodfire pizza place had better rations and a much better atmosphere, but I had such high expectations that I could only be critical instead of recognizing the good food that I was eating. Instead of having an enjoyable experience at a delightful restaurant, I had a mediocre experience, criticizing food that I should have enjoyed more than I did.

Expectations shape how we respond to people and situations, and they can often create trouble that wouldn't be there otherwise.

I think expectations are part of the trouble that we Christians create for ourselves when we talk to non-Christians individually and to society as a whole. To explore this, let's go back a couple of millennia. What was it like to be a Christian in the first century, and how was that different from today? What did they expect from the world, and what did the world expect from them? Have you ever thought about this?

The early believers had to find their way in a world where "the Church" was essentially unknown and completely outside of the authority and power structures of the ancient world.

They could expect almost nothing from their culture; they couldn't expect people to understand their language or the foundation of their community. Some Romans even reported that early Christians were "cannibals" for "eating the body and blood of Jesus." But that kind of cultural misunderstanding was to be expected. After all, no one but the first followers of Jesus knew what it meant to be in a church who believed that the same God who raised Israel up from Egypt raised his own crucified Son from the dead by the Spirit. When it came to the broader culture they lived in, the early church had pretty low expectations.

Today, in contrast, our expectations for culture can be quite high—especially if we grew up in established denominational churches. In fact, I wonder whether our ingrained expectations aren't a sizeable part of the problem with how we relate to our culture. Many of us expect that American culture is going to resonate with our Christian values, and recognize quickly the truth of God's Word.

These expectations are only heightened by the fact that, not so long ago, North American culture was dominated by Christian language and thinking that permeated even political speech and the educational system. It feels like so many people used to believe in Jesus as the Savior and wanted to embody Christian morals; and now, the situation has changed dramatically.

Our faith is sometimes rejected out of hand, and we feel dismayed when we speak our Christian language and people are put off. We feel hurt when the culture does not support—or even respect—our Christian ways of being and living.

But why should we expect a non-Christian culture and people who have no connection to Jesus to agree with God's Word on any particular issue or value? Why would people who have never lived in the community of the Church understand sin, holiness, grace, or salvation? Why would we expect people who have never submitted themselves to

Holy Scripture to find common ground with us easily on matters of Christian conviction?

We shouldn't be surprised when atheists or agnostics disagree with us, or more importantly, with Scripture; but we should find joy, and rejoice with the angels in heaven, when they do hear the Word of God and believe it. **Faith, after all, is no less than a miracle, accomplished by God alone.**

Consider again the expectations of the early church. What did the disciples in Acts expect? The apostles seemed to expect (or were at least not surprised by) persecution, suffering, and challenges from the establishment as religious leaders tried to shut them up (Acts 4:15–22, 5:17–42, 7:54–8:3), political leaders threw them in prison (Acts 12:6–19, 16:25–40), and mobs even kicked them out of cities as they preached and taught the Gospel (Acts 13:50–51, 14:4–6, 14:19, 17:13–14, 19:21–41).

At the same time, though, those first followers also came to expect the Holy Spirit to work through normal words about Jesus, through preaching and teaching that Jesus is the Messiah and the resurrected Son of God (Acts 3:41–47, 6:7, 10:44–48, 11:18, 15:12–21, 16:14–15).

These believers wanted to show how Jesus connected with the vast variety of people from many and various cultures, proclaiming that Jesus wanted to make them all a part of his story and work in the world. For some, who understood Israel, the message of Jesus as the Messiah of God, the promised King, made sense (Acts 13:16–41). For others, the apostles proclaimed Jesus as the Son of God, sent by the Creator to judge all people, evidenced by his death and resurrection (Acts 17:22–31).

Throughout the book of Acts, you see many disciples tailoring a message of grace to diverse people in a variety of cultures, always with Jesus at the center. **What you do *not* see is the disciples expecting to get a hearing just because they were talking about Christian morals or teachings.** Why do we expect that today?

If we can find a way to reset our expectations, maybe we could learn again with the apostles and the early church that **human power does not make the Church.** Jesus establishes and preserves the Church himself—and against our own expectations, Jesus does things his way: the way of the cross.

Matthew 16:24-28 (Peter: "The cross will never happen to you!" Jesus: "Get behind me, Satan!") follows quickly on the heels of Matthew 16:16-18 (Peter: "You are the Christ, the Son of the living God." Jesus: "On this rock I will build my Church.") for a reason! Jesus builds his Church in ways we would never guess without the Spirit and often fail to recognize.

If we can find a way to reset our expectations, maybe we could learn again that the Holy Spirit is at work to build a living temple that is the

Church out of "those who are near" as well as "those who were far off" (Ephesians 2:14-22), despite and beyond our own assumptions and presuppositions. If we can find a way to reset our expectations, maybe we could learn again that we do not need *cultural power* to bring the power of God; rather, **we need plain words about Jesus, shown in the context of a life well-lived according to God's design.** This is what the Church has always confessed: the word of Christ is the power of God to salvation for everyone who believes.

How do we reset our expectations? Do two things: first, **expect *less* from the world and what they think of us**; second, **expect *more* from our God** and the power of the word of Christ to change the world (and us, too!). Don't expect too much from the world, but expect everything from plain words about Jesus. Then hold on and enjoy the ride!

12. Empowered to Hear

By Justin Rossow

Today we celebrated my niece Karolein's confirmation as well as her 15th birthday with a special party, the traditional *Quinceañera*. As part of the ceremony, family and friends got to give gifts of special meaning and share a word of encouragement for the birthday girl, as she stands on the cusp of womanhood.

My immediate family had the task of giving birthstone earrings with a blessing and a reminder to listen to God's Word.

Thinking about what to say, or which of the many Bible verses about God's Word I could use, I recalled an unusual text from an Old Testament lesson used in worship earlier this summer. I remembered it was July 4th because of the irony involved: the pastor preached on our dependence on Jesus while our country celebrated Independence Day.

(In my daily calendar where I take brief notes or sketch an image from what I saw in God's Word that day, I have crossed out the *In-* and simply marked it *Dependence Day*, which for followers of Jesus, is a holiday we get to celebrate year round.)

I remembered that July 4 verse, so I was able to go back and find the actual text read that day in worship. The Old Testament lesson that day came from the second chapter of Ezekiel.

In Ezekiel 1, the young prophet sees a vision of the glory of the LORD that knocks him down to the ground. Then, in the opening verses of Ezekiel 2, we get these words (my translation):

> Then [the LORD] commanded me: "Son of Adam, stand up on your feet and I will speak my Word to you." And the Spirit/Wind/Breath entered into me as he spoke the Word to me; and the Spirit set me on my feet, and I heard the One who was speaking his Word to me."
>
> *Ezekiel 2:1-2 (JPR)*

I love the dependence embedded in this verse. Ezekiel is face down in the presence of God and is told to stand on his own two feet to hear the Word of the LORD. I wanted to say the same thing to my niece on her Quinceañera: I wanted her to stand firm and listen always to God's Word.

But the Spirit, who works both the desire and the ability in us to do the things that bring God delight, doesn't simply leave Ezekiel (or Karolein, or you, or me) with a command–even a command to receive God's Word–without the help we need to enact the command.

We joyfully rely on God's promises without having to depend on our own strength to trust or understand or believe (and without taking any credit for our trust or understanding or faith). We get to receive the promise with open hands, hands that were given to us in the first place; hands that the Spirit pries open again and again when they are closed in anger or selfishness or stubbornness or pride. We get to lean into dependence on Jesus, a dependence that is given, shaped, and empowered by the very breath of God.

So Ezekiel (and Karolein and you and I) receive a command to receive, and even that invitation comes with power from God to receive the invitation. The Spirit (or breath or wind) of God enters into the prophet and brings about what God commands. With the Word comes the Spirit. The Spirit stands Ezekiel on his feet, so that he is able to hear the Word and the One speaking.

So my encouragement for Karo is a promise I hold onto again today. I invite you into that promise, trusting that the Spirit is able to empower your dependence, to stand you on your feet so you can hear and receive a promise and command to hear and receive.

"The LORD commanded me, stand on your feet and I will speak to you, and the Spirit entered into me, and the Spirit stood me on my feet, and I heard."

Karolein, may these birthstone earrings remind you always to listen and hold onto God's Word of promise. And may they also remind you of the Spirit who enters into you by the power of that Word, and enables you to stand, and to hear.

God grant this unto us all. Amen.

13. Where is Jesus Speaking?

By Justin Rossow

Ask even a faithful follower what Jesus has been speaking into their life lately, and you should expect to get a blank stare. *What do you mean, "What has Jesus been speaking into my life??" Does Jesus actually speak to me? How would I even know? Is this a trick question??*

The Monday before classes started last fall, my daughter Kate was feeling kind of anxious about her first day of high school. My kids are some of the people who help me follow Jesus, so I asked her, "What has Jesus been speaking into your life lately?"

She was more than willing to play along, but she had no place to begin: "How would I know what Jesus is speaking to me about starting high school?" Fair question.

So I prompted her. "Well, I think you were sitting next to me as we listened to a sermon yesterday," I said. "Did any of that apply to you, do you think?" Of course, I had my three things from the sermon I wanted her to remember (no, I wasn't preaching that day) but I thought it would be better if it came from her.

"The *sermon*??" Kate asked. "You mean, the sermon *counts*??"

I'm not sure what she thought I was asking. Did she think I thought Jesus was going to leave her a voicemail, or send a private message on Snapchat? No idea. But once she knew I was asking what she heard in worship, or what she had been reading in her Bible, or any of the *normal* places you might find God's Word, she at least had a place to begin.

In fact, Kate went on to list not only two of my three main thoughts from the sermon, but about six other connections I hadn't thought of yet. I just made encouraging noises once in a while (and took some notes) while she talked herself out of being nervous about high school and into trusting God's presence in her life. I count that as a parenting win: Kate was much better at applying Sunday's sermon to her Monday problem than I would have been. But she needed me to help get her started.

Ask *what* Jesus is speaking, and you often get blank stares. Ask *where* is Jesus speaking, and people begin to notice places where God's Word shows up in their ordinary week.

There's the sermon (yes, that counts!), and the podcast you listen to; the thing your friend told you they read in the Bible that morning, and the Portals of Prayer that sits in a high-traffic area in your house. You got an email from a family member, and you were still humming a hymn from worship in the car, and your fourth-grader needed help with some Sunday School memory work. You looked at a couple of notes you took on the back of last weekend's worship folder before you recycled it, you skimmed a Facebook post from one of your favorite Christian authors, and you did manage to read your Bible twice this week!

When you start looking for God's Word to show up in your life, you start to hear the voice of Jesus speaking in, with, and under the voice of the preacher, the blog writer, the devotional author, and your friend. That's when you start noticing what Jesus has been saying to you over and over again, all week long. Wondering *where* leads quite naturally to noticing *what*.

In the month of January, I kept a calendar of words, phrases, or images that helped me remember the Word of God I encountered each day (a practice that came from my friends at Visual Faith™ Ministry). Looking back on a month of capturing key concepts from God's Word, I see not only *what* Jesus has been speaking into my life, but *where*.

I finished Luke in 2021 and started reading the Gospel of Mark daily in 2022, though looking back on January, I didn't actually read Mark *daily*: plenty of times other places in Scripture demanded my attention. But Mark was always the rhythm I had to fall back on if I didn't have something more pressing.

I preached a lot in January, and wrote some blogs for the Craft of Preaching, so the verses that were on my heart and mind for those showed up in my own personal devotional life. I also captured verses other people shared with me in a staff meeting, or on a podcast or, yes, in a sermon. One of the things I wrote on my Key Concept Calendar came from a men's coffee shop Bible study; one came from a Facebook Live devotion; and another even came from a gift mailed to me by a friend.

Of course, verses from Mark keep weaving in and out of my calendar, but I was amazed to see *how many different places* the Spirit used to put God's Word into the path of my ordinary, everyday life. Those places Jesus was speaking were all there before I noticed them; but noticing *where* Jesus is speaking helps me pay attention to *what* Jesus is speaking in my life. I'm kind of looking forward to February!

14. Paul's Letter of Recommendation

By Conrad Gempf

If you want to understand the difficulties Paul had in his relationship with the church he founded in Corinth, 2 Corinthians 3:1-6 tells you almost everything you need to know.

> Are we beginning to commend ourselves again? Or do we need, like some people, letters of recommendation to you or from you? You yourselves are our letter, written on our hearts, known and read by everyone. You show that you are a letter from Christ, the result of our ministry, written not with ink but with the Spirit of the living God, not on tablets of stone but on tablets of human hearts.
>
> Such confidence we have through Christ before God. Not that we are competent in ourselves to claim anything for ourselves, but our competence comes from God. He has made us competent as ministers of a new covenant—not of the letter but of the Spirit; for the letter kills, but the Spirit gives life.
>
> *2 Corinthians 3:1-6 (NIV)*

2 Corinthians is an emotionally turbulent letter, and many of the issues are hinted at here at the beginning of chapter 3. Essentially, the Apostle Paul seems to desire and even expect a relationship with Corinthians that is full of trust and respect. Instead, Paul finds himself

thought ill of — unjustly, he feels — and ends up discouraged as well as angry at being made to feel that he needs to justify his actions and status. (Which he does, by the way: in 2 Corinthians 1:16–2:1, for example, Paul takes pains to explain why he did not visit the Corinthians as he'd planned.)

Paul's first rhetorical question in 2 Corinthians 3:1 relates to this explaining himself: do I have to keep defending my actions? That the apostle should need "letters of recommendation" which he refers to next is, of course, absurd. Then as now, letters of recommendation are *only needed by strangers*—before the two parties involved know each other. The Corinthian believers should know Paul better than that!

Such letters were common in the Ancient World, among both Jews and Gentiles. Two obvious New Testament examples of letters of recommendation are the documents the young Saul of Tarsus received from the High Priest to justify work that he wanted to do in Damascus (Acts 9:1-2), and, more pointedly, the Corinthians will have received such letters concerning Apollos from the church in Ephesus (Acts 18:27). Paul is probably not referring to either of these letters particularly, but they demonstrate the kind of thing he has in mind.

Paul then escalates the matter from trivial explanations, rationalizations, and formulaic reference letters. In a masterstroke of rhetorical strategy, Paul manages to flatter the Corinthians as well as himself. "YOU are our letter of recommendation..."

Paul is saying, "You guys are so good, you make ME look good in front of everyone else, including the Lord!" How amazing, to be able to tell them they are *wrong* by telling them they are *good*! Of course, these positive words concentrate on the overall effect of their relationship with Paul, and thus urge them to move on from trivial matters of missed visits and so on.

The pair of contrasts that ensue in verse 3 are also remarkable. Paul expands and deepens the theme of written reference letters—not ink but Spirit; not stone but hearts—making a subtle reference to the very nature of Christian faith. Our faith is not about written stipulations, or contracts, or Law (hence the "tablets of stone") but about the heart and about relationship.

The next paragraph foreshadows the more aggressive elements of Paul's defense of his apostolic authority in 2 Corinthians 10-13, but also displays his own internal struggle between confidence and humility, which will be a hallmark of the whole book (even to the extreme of the ecstatic vision and thorn in the flesh in 12:1-10).

Although this *humble confidence* is undoubtedly true of Paul himself, this attitude of the heart is also what he wishes to see in the Corinthian believers. This humble confidence contrasts with his opponents' boasting, which Paul will lampoon later in the letter (see especially 10:12-18).

2 Corinthians 3:1-6 is a remarkable window not only into Paul's difficulties with these people but also into his attempts to be reconciled with them. I find it comforting that Paul went through frustrations with fellow-believers, just as I sometimes do. I also find Paul's example an encouragement to seek reconciliation with other people through being positive (even if I also sometimes resort to sarcasm, like Paul does. See 11:19-21).

Dear Jesus, Lord of the Church,
I lift up my faith relationships to you today,
especially those that seem fragile or strained.

Where my own stubborn will or hard heart
has added to the discord,
forgive me and renew me.

Where it lies within my power
to restore or renew a relationship,
guide me and use me.

Send your Spirit into my heart.
Give me a humble confidence
that celebrates my relationship
with other people who belong to you. Amen.

15. Why am I so Thirsty?

By Justin Rossow

As dropsies, though filled with fluid, crave drink,
so money-lovers, though loaded with money, crave more of it;
yet both to their own demise.

—Diogenes the Cynic (ca 300 BC)

One Sabbath day after worship (in Luke 14), Jesus is invited over to dinner at the house of a local Pharisee. Other prominent religious leaders round out the guest list, making this a gathering of the religiously well-trained and well-practiced; a kind of Sunday luncheon for elders, pastors, and theology professors.

An uninvited guest also shows up: a man suffering from a condition called "dropsy." More of a symptom than a disease, dropsy causes your body to retain water to the point of serious harm or even death. But here's the kicker: a dropsy is always thirsty. This man can't get enough of what's killing him.

Some 300 years before the dinner party in Luke 14, the Greek philosopher Diogenes the Cynic wrote: "As dropsies, though filled with fluid, crave drink, so money-lovers, though loaded with money, crave more of it; yet both to their own demise."

That's the physical condition of the unwelcome guest at the Pharisee's religious reception. It turns out, it's also the spiritual condition of so many of these good, religious leaders gathered for the feast.

Did you know the Pharisees are good, religious people? They get kind of a bad rap in the Gospels, but Pharisees are only the bad guys because their good, religious lives don't have any room for Jesus.

The Pharisees knew their Bible. They read Scripture more often than we do, and had more Bible verses memorized than you or I would even dare to attempt. The Pharisees prayed, like a lot. And they prayed well (and liked it when people heard them pray such good prayers so often). The Pharisees gave generously (though the Gospel of Luke does identify them as money-lovers), donating 10% of their entire income, down to the mint leaves from their garden boxes (and they liked it when you knew how generously and meticulously they gave).

Did you know that Pharisees were such good, religious people that they held the equivalent of Outreach and Evangelism Conferences? The Pharisees actually wanted the lost to be saved. Their outreach strategy was simple: live good, religious lives so well—and display the benefits of living good, religious lives so clearly—that sinners out there would see the good life, give up on their sinful ways, and join the club reserved for good, religious people.

Jesus had a very different strategy: go hang out with sinners. Sparks usually flew when Jesus and the Pharisees got together, in part because they were both after the eternal souls of the very same people, but had very different ideas about how to reach them and bring them into the fold.

The Pharisees would never welcome a dropsy to their religious luncheon, not because they were bad people, but because they were so good. Dropsy makes you unclean by Levitical law, unfit for the presence of God, and eating with someone who is unclean makes you unclean, too. Interacting with a dropsy would not only ruin their theological lunch, it could prevent them from fulfilling certain religious duties for a time. So when Jesus engages this man with dropsy, the religious bystanders are on pins and needles; this could go very bad, very fast.

Then Jesus asks them if it's lawful to heal on the Sabbath or not! These Pharisees don't have an answer, not because they are so depraved, but because they are so concerned about being good. They not only followed the religious laws around the Sabbath, that covenant sign of their relationship with God, they made extra rules around the Sabbath laws just to make sure they stayed in-bounds. Now this Jesus guy is looking for Sabbath loop-holes? What kind of trouble is he trying to stir up?

Jesus, saddened and frustrated by their hard, religious hearts, heals the thirsty man with dropsy and sends him away. Then Jesus turns his attention to the Pharisees, the spiritual dropsies at his dinner table.

Jesus notices how they all want the best, most honored seats at the table. (After all, good lives reap good rewards, and the only way to show sinners how good the good life can be is to gain very public recognition for being good.) Jesus has a different idea: make yourself low and humble, because God raises up the lowly. Don't throw religious parties for the religious people who can pay you back; invite the low, humble, unclean—people who can't pay back your goodness with their own. That's how God's Kingdom works.

Jesus' call to humility is met with another round of boasting. With eyes blinded by self-righteousness and ears plugged by his own pride, one of the fine, upstanding guests responds to all this talk about banquets by saying, "How blessed are the people [like me, of course] who will get to eat and drink in the Kingdom of God!"

Like spiritual dropsies, these good, religious people are choking on their own religiosity, all the while craving more and more of the self-righteousness in which they are drowning.

So Jesus tries again. This time the punchline of the parable is a direct threat to the self-righteousness and self-confidence of these spiritual dropsies: none of the invited guests get to taste a morsel of the King's banquet, even though they RSVP'd yes.

Their rejection of their relationship with the King leaves them out in the cold, stuck with their own pride and self-sufficiency. Those who sit down to eat and drink in the Kingdom are the blind, the lame, the unclean people (like the man with dropsy) who aren't good enough to come in. Even people who are outside of the community, people who live out where the foreigners and sinners and, well, *outsiders* live—they are gently taken by the hand and escorted into the banquet over their own objections that they aren't worthy enough, they aren't good enough, they can't repay this grace.

And that, ultimately, is the point. The ones who know they don't deserve the invitation and can't repay the generosity of the King, they are the ones who get to sit down at table and eat and drink in the Kingdom. Self-sufficient, self-righteous, self-aggrandizing spiritual dropsies—filled to the brim with their own religiosity, but craving even more—need not apply.

The water a dropsy craves is deadly, not because the water is bad, but because a disease makes it poisonous. The good, religious activities—like prayer, or fasting, or Scripture reading, or worship—that these good, religious Pharisees crave are to them a poison, not because these religious disciplines are bad, but because they are feeding a self-righteous self-sufficiency that doesn't need Jesus.

That kind of spiritual disease, a kind of religious dropsy, is a danger for anyone who tries to take faith seriously. By wanting to grow in your faith, by wanting to take a next step, by desiring a more faithful walk, and living out your faith, you become susceptible to one of the most devious tricks in the tempter's arsenal: your religious activity can insulate you from needing Jesus.

How do you know when you have been infected with the kind of self-righteous self-sufficiency that can kill your faith? Maybe it's hard to tell all on your own; maybe you need a trusted friend to help in your own diagnosis. But I think a continual thirst for more may be a kind of early warning system.

If you are working hard at taking a next step, if you are active, and engaged, and reading Scripture, and praying, and paying attention in worship, and serving in the community and serving at your local congregation, and you look around at all the good, religious things you are doing, and you feel exhausted, but at the same time, you think you should be doing more… Well, that's kind of normal. And it may also be a sign that you are getting so religious that religion is getting in the way of Jesus.

If you do all the right spiritual things, and your calendar is chock full of spiritual activities, and you still find yourself asking, "Why am I so spiritually thirsty all the time?" it could be that a kind of spiritual dropsy has set in.

If all the external trappings of a Christian culture give you a sense of value or maybe even pride, but they don't drive you to needing Jesus, maybe you are so full of Christian *religion* that you are in danger of drowning.

You aren't alone. Don't despair. Take it to Jesus.

I find great comfort in the fact that the Apostle Paul *was a Pharisee* before Jesus knocked him off his donkey. Jesus heals even spiritual dropsies. Jesus heals even me.

The answer to spiritual dropsy and religious workaholism is not to try harder or to do better. The answer also isn't to give up on doing good, religious things and try to be more *sinful*, so you need more forgiveness. ("Shall we sin more so grace may abound more? Are you nuts??" [Romans 6:1-2, loose translation].)

The answer Jesus gives to the people who are burdened with their own spiritual pride is quite simple: get back to desperately needing Jesus.

In John 7, Jesus says, "Let anyone who is thirsty *come to me* and drink!" The last parable in Luke 14 ends with the outcasts being led by the Messenger of the Invitation to sit down to eat and drink with the King at the banquet table. The answer to too much religious self-sufficiency isn't more religion. It certainly isn't more sin. It's just *more Jesus*.

Keep reading your Bible; and let the Bible drive you to deeper dependence on Jesus. Keep praying, more and more often: and make your prayers a desperate cry for more Jesus in your life. Work hard (with a friend) to find and take a next step, run a faith experiment, try something new, engage the adventure of discipleship; and at every turn, let every discovery, every act of courage or exploration be driven by a deep need for the presence and the grace of Jesus in your everyday walk.

Don't get so good at taking a next step that you forget about following Jesus. And if you do find all this religious work is leaving you dry and thirsty, don't just try harder. And don't just give up. Do what the dropsy in Luke 14 did: go find Jesus, and trust his healing.

Reading this far in a blog on discipleship is a rather dangerous thing; you could start feeling pretty good about yourself. As you get "better" at following Jesus, remember that one of the best ways to describe "discipleship" is simply this: *discipleship is growing more and more in the understanding of how much you need Jesus all the time, for absolutely everything.*

Don't be shocked or surprised if you discover you've fallen into a habit of spiritual self-sufficiency; it happens even to the best followers; or, rather, *especially* to the *best* followers. Jesus loves you so much, he will show up at your dropsy party or knock you off your donkey if that's what it takes to bring you back into a posture of dependence, a posture that receives the Kingdom the only way the Kingdom can be received: as a gift.

16. It is Finished; and ...

By Justin Rossow

I recently received some concerned feedback about a devotion I wrote in *When from Death I'm Free: A Hymn Journal for Holy Week.* I love hearing from readers because it makes me think carefully about what I am saying; it also helps me see what's on the hearts and minds of people I am trying to serve.

The phrase in question came in a devotion on 1 Corinthians 15, where I said, in part: **"His [Jesus'] work isn't fully finished. His victory is not yet completely complete."** My reader put those words next to John 19:30 and Jesus' cry, **"It is finished!"** and expressed some concern ... and I think I see where she is coming from.

If I thought someone were taking away from the completeness of Jesus' work on the cross—or if I thought someone were talking about the cross in a way that left something for me to do to be saved, or that diminished the power and comfort of the words, "It is finished," I'm sure I would feel the need to speak up as well.

In the context of John 19:30, I would never say Jesus' work isn't finished. When Jesus says on the cross, "It is finished!" everything necessary for Jesus to suffer is done. Jesus is finished with the role of Suffering Servant.

The sacrifice of Jesus and work of forgiveness won by his blood stands forever in a permanent, completed state: you don't need to (and, in fact, can't) add to the fulfilled sacrifice of Jesus.

You can be confident you are forgiven and take comfort in the fact that you are saved by grace as a free gift, without adding to Jesus' work on the cross. The sacrifice is complete.

With that sacrificial lens in mind, the author to the Hebrews can even call the death of Jesus a kind of victory:

> He [Jesus] too shared in their humanity so that **by his death**
> he might destroy him who holds the power of death—that is,
> the devil—and free those who all their lives were held in
> slavery by their fear of death.

> *Hebrews 2:14-15 (NIV)*

If you want to know if the price for your sin has been completely paid, or if the debt you owe to God has been completely done away with, or if your sins are completely forgiven, then **turn to John 19:30 and trust Jesus when he says, "It is finished!"**

The story isn't over, however, when they put Jesus in the tomb. The sacrifice is complete, and Jesus is still active. Of course, Jesus is going to rise again on the Third Day. The resurrection was not yet complete in John 19:30; but the "IT" in "It is finished" has to do with suffering and sacrifice in a way that the resurrection does not.

So in John 19:30, Jesus' suffering and sacrificial death are complete; in John 20, Jesus rises from the dead. **The work of the cross is finished; and Jesus is still at work, for us.**

The Bible has more than one faithful way of talking about the work of Jesus for us, and we want to be faithful to the whole of Scripture. The context of Jesus' words on the cross are important; and we should trust and believe and take comfort in the words, "It is finished."

We also want to elevate the work of Jesus in his resurrection. In fact, Paul can go so far as to say, if you only believe that Jesus died for you and not that he rose again for you, you don't actually have the full story:

Now if Christ is proclaimed as raised from the dead, how can
some of you say that there is no resurrection of the dead?
But if there is no resurrection of the dead, then not even Christ
has been raised. And if Christ has not been raised, then our
preaching is in vain and your faith is in vain… And if Christ has
not been raised, your faith is futile and you are still in your sins.

1 Corinthians 15:12-14, 17 (ESV)

1 Corinthians 15 would *not* be the right context to say that *everything Jesus did was completed on the cross,* because some of the people in Corinth were taking that completed work to mean that Jesus didn't actually rise, and the resurrection of the dead is unnecessary.

I'm pretty sure Paul believes John 19:30, and yet he can say that the resurrection of Jesus is still important for your salvation. That doesn't mean that 1 Corinthians 15 is refuting John 19; it just means we want to read any Bible verse in its context.

The Scriptures invite you to take comfort in the fact that the sacrifice of Jesus was complete on the cross and that you don't have to add to it. The Scriptures also invite you to take comfort in the fact that Jesus rose from the dead for you, and that your victory over death is assured. Finally, the Scriptures invite you to take comfort in the fact that Jesus is coming again for you and the dead will rise, and you also will see that final victory over death with your own resurrection eyes.

That's the context of my words: **"So as long as any human body of someone Jesus loves lies in a grave, Jesus isn't content. His work isn't fully finished. His victory is not yet completely complete."** That devotion comes directly after the hymn journal quotes 1 Corinthians 15:24-26:

Then comes the end, when he delivers the kingdom to God
the Father after destroying every rule and every authority and
power. For [Jesus] must reign until he has put all his enemies
under his feet. The last enemy to be destroyed is death.

1 Corinthians 15:24-26 (ESV)

Here, Paul says the final victory is not yet won until the last enemy, death, is destroyed. And from this perspective of the resurrection of the dead and the life of the world to come, that ultimate, final, consummate victory doesn't come at the cross or even at Jesus' empty tomb, but when death is done away with forever on the Last Day.

Paul is not contradicting Hebrews 2:14-15 that called Jesus' *death* a victory over death; nor is the Last Day victory over death (1 Corinthians 15:26) contradicting 1 Corinthians 15:21, where Paul says that the resurrection of Jesus on the Third Day means that the resurrection of the dead has already come to all humanity.

The death of Jesus on the cross defeated death; *and* the resurrection of Jesus on the Third Day defeated death; *AND* Death is the last enemy to be destroyed on the Last Day, when Jesus returns in glory to judge both the living and the dead. In other words, Good Friday defeats death; the Third Day defeats death; and the Last Day defeats death once and for all. That's the ancient creed of the Church: **Christ has died; Christ is risen; Christ will come again.**

The faithful woman who asked about my statement that Jesus' work isn't fully finished was reading John 19:30 and was concerned about comfort and confidence. I am, too. If you are suffering from a guilty conscience and you want to know if you can possibly do enough to be worthy of forgiveness, I want you to be confident that **the sacrifice of Jesus on the cross is complete: you don't have to add anything to it.**

You can't add to what Jesus did. *Jesus is finished with his work.* You are forgiven. You are free. At the same time, if you are grieving, if you or someone you know has received a terminal diagnosis, if you are standing at the graveside of someone you love, I want you to be confident in the fact that J*esus is not yet done working.*

Take comfort in the fact that death isn't the final word. **Jesus loves your body. Jesus died for your body. Your body is going to rise.** And *Jesus will not stop his work* until the last enemy, death, has been destroyed once and for all.

These two things are both true: (1) it is good news that the work of Jesus is finished, and I am forgiven; and (2) it is good news that Jesus is not done working, and death will not be allowed to stand.

If I understood my concerned reader correctly, I think she was trying to say (1); if so, I agree with her. In my devotion, I was trying to say (2). I think Paul agrees with me. I hope you can see how (1) and (2) are not contradictory: **both are true words of comfort for different contexts.**

Don't tell a repentant sinner that the work of Jesus isn't finished. And don't tell a grieving widow that Jesus is done working, and there is nothing left for her.

I believe that the sacrifice of Jesus stands completed, once for all; and I believe in the resurrection of the dead and the life of the world to come. Both bring me immense comfort.

17. When Good Friday Feels Like Failure

By Justin Rossow

Of course, we know the big picture. We have the benefit of hindsight, and we know that the open tomb is just around the corner. Of course, Jesus—true God, begotten of the Father before all worlds, very God of Very God—isn't bound by time: Jesus himself has been announcing both his own death and his bodily resurrection way before Good Friday and Easter Sunday.

Of course, we know—and Jesus knows—that he is the Lamb of God who takes away the sin of the world (John 1), that by his death he destroys death (Hebrews 2), that Jesus has authority both to lay down his life and to take it up again (John 10).

But I don't think it *felt* like that to Jesus in the moment. And it certainly doesn't always feel like that to people who belong to Jesus.

I have been told by some good, well-meaning Christians that God has never let them down, that they have never had more than they could handle, that their faith has never wavered and even their trials are sweet.

On my good days, I accept this at face value and thank God that they have been blessed with an experience we have never been promised and could change (any minute now). On my bad days, I wonder who they are trying to fool and what they are hiding, maybe even from themselves. But on most days, I simply think that if God has never seemed to let you down, you're either not paying attention or you're not trying hard enough.

We have lots of promises from God, some temporal and some eternal. Whether God is faithful to the eternal promises will only be demonstrated in eternity; I trust Jesus is faithful, and some day, my faith will be sight.

But even before the resurrection of the dead and the life of the age to come, we are invited to know and trust God as Father, Shepherd, King, Refuge, Fortress, even Friend. You can see how, like a caring shepherd, God provides and protects and leads and guides.

Except when God doesn't.

And that's the problem of trying to live out what we know about God in the seemingly arbitrary experiences of life in a broken and fallen world.

You might know the big picture, that death is not the final word, that your sins will not keep you from God's presence, that even though your world falls apart, you have a promise stronger than the world. At a macro level, you trust God's promises; *but why does it feel like God isn't coming through in my day to day experience?*

What do you do when God doesn't seem to be acting like a Father, Shepherd, King, Refuge, Fortress, or even Friend?

I think we find a kind of answer on Good Friday—not in seeing Jesus as the Lamb of God who destroys death and who will rise again in three short days, but in seeing Jesus, abandoned by God, and trusting anyway.

Jesus clearly has a promise from God. (Let's think for a moment *from below*; that is, let's acknowledge that Jesus is one with the Father, but set his divinity aside for a moment, just like Jesus did on the cross.)

Jesus, from his own human perspective, knows he has been declared God's own beloved Son. Jesus has received the Spirit, and in the power of the Spirit, Jesus has experienced God's Kingdom breaking into the world. Jesus is confident that he is fulfilling his Father's commands and abiding in his Father's love (John 15). Jesus knows he is going to go through severe suffering, but he also knows the Father's will is going to be done. Jesus is living out his trust in his Father's love.

And then comes the cross.

At the cross, God's promises seem to fail. We know the rest of the story, so we know they didn't *really* fail. But *the experience of God's failure* is all too real, even for Jesus.

"My God, my God—why have you abandoned me?" Jesus cries in anguish. The Mighty Fortress didn't protect. The Friend has become an Enemy. Where is the Father now?

Jesus knows that Sunday is coming; but Friday is here, and here in force. Do you know what that's like?

It's true: Jesus rescues us from our sin and from God's judgment. We who were once far off and God's enemies are now, by the power of the cross, brought near and adopted into the family: God's beloved daughters; God's beloved sons. You have that promise. You know that promise. You can trust that promise.

And, as long as you still live in a broken and sinful world, you will still experience what feels like your own Good Fridays. You will still experience separation from God. As soon as you trust that God's promises matter, not just for eternity, but for your everyday life, you will get to know what it means to feel let down by God.

What do you do when God doesn't seem to be acting like a Father, Shepherd, King, Refuge, Fortress, or even Friend?

Look to the man on the cross. In Jesus on the cross you see not only the Lamb of God who takes away the sin of the world and beats death at its own game, you also see the Artist's rendering, the Architect's blueprint, the Potter's design for you and for your life of faith. You see the kind of trust the Spirit of the Living God is shaping and forming in you.

As the Spirit joins you to Jesus and conforms you more and more to the image of Christ, this is the faith the Spirit has in mind. You have been crucified with Christ and you no longer live, but Christ lives in you. The normal, ordinary, everyday life you now live in the body you live by faith in the Son of God, the same Son who felt abandoned by the Father when he needed God most.

When Jesus experiences the mystery of God's absence on Good Friday, what do we see him do? Although Jesus knows and trusts this isn't the end of the story, it sure feels like it is; and Jesus let's God know exactly what he's feeling.

Jesus isn't afraid to look like he doesn't trust God's promises; he simply let's God know that those promises don't seem to be doing much good right now. "Why have you forsaken me? That's not what you are supposed to do! That's not what you promised!"

Jesus calls out to God even when God feels far away.

How often do I hide my own experience of being let down by God, even from myself? It seems like my own personal failure in faith to feel like God has failed me in even the smallest detail.

If I feel abandoned in the ordinary details of my life, surely the promise of life and resurrection should be big enough to cheer me up and take away my pain, right? If I had enough faith, this wouldn't seem so bad, right?

But Jesus doesn't think like that. Easter Sunday does not eclipse the real suffering of the cross. If anything, it works the other way around: the impossibly large stone of the garden tomb has rolled in front of God's promises and blotted out the sun.

Jesus isn't ashamed to feel forsaken by God; and in his abandonment, *Jesus turns to God*. That's part of the response to suffering the Spirit is shaping in you. When it feels like God has let you down, the Spirit leads you back to God.

The Spirit shapes the faithful prayer of Jesus on your lips, even when it feels like prayers are wasted and faith is futile: "My God, my God, why have you abandoned me? Where are your promises now, God? What kind of Father are you?"

I'm somewhat threatened by that response, since that prayer can feel like I no longer trust or no longer believe, or that I have, by my own failure, lost sight of the big picture.

But sometimes Good Friday does eclipse Easter in the life of God's beloved sons and daughters. And when that happens, pouring out your fear and anger and hurt and disappointment and abandonment in prayer is a faithful response.

Go back and read Psalm 22—the Psalm of David that starts, *"My God, my God, why have you forsaken me? Why are you so far from saving me, from the words of my groaning?"*—go back and read that whole psalm and you will find the very real experience of abandonment intertwined with trust and confidence in God in spite of the fact that God feels, for the moment, far away.

In Jesus on the cross, you see that kind of stubborn trust in God's promises, even when they seem to fail. Even at the very end, Jesus addresses the God who feels like an enemy as *Father*.

Even at the very end, Jesus entrusts himself to God, even though, for the moment, it feels like God is unable or unwilling to save. *"Father,"* Jesus prays at the very end, "Father, into your hands I commend my spirit."

Part of the foolishness and scandal of the cross is a trust in God as Father, even when all the Father's promises have seemed to fail. And that's the faith the Spirit of Jesus is shaping in you.

Please understand: I am not asking you to *try harder* to emulate the faith of Jesus on the cross. I am not telling you, in your moment of fear or doubt or pain, when the promise you thought you had from God has failed miserably and you feel not only let down but abandoned—in that Good Friday experience, I am not asking you to try harder to be like Jesus. I'm not even telling you to remember Easter. The Resurrection is just around the corner, and it will make all the difference in the world, but Friday's here; and, for now, Sunday feels like it may never arrive.

When you enter into your own Good Friday experience, look to the man on the cross. Hear his cry, "Why?" Lean in to hear him pray, *"Father..."* And know that the Spirit who lives in you is shaping your faith to look like that.

Don't try harder; look for the Spirit to work. Don't hide from your experience of God's failure; let God know exactly what you are experiencing. Don't abandon the God who seems to have abandoned you; commit your life to your Heavenly Father even when that seems like an empty thing to do.

If you have honestly never had an experience where it seemed like God's promises failed you, thank God for that grace. And if you have only ever trusted God for your eternal salvation and never thought to trust

God to be your Father, Shepherd, King, Refuge, Fortress, or even Friend for the needs and concerns of your everyday life, there is a world of joy and dependence I would invite you to explore. But trusting God's promises in your everyday life comes with a risk. Those promises sometimes feel like they fail. You don't have to be afraid of that experience, or hide that experience (from yourself or from God). Easter is strong enough to defeat each and every one of your Good Fridays.

And even Good Friday has its own kind of beauty and hope. On Good Friday we see the kind of faith the Spirit is shaping in us, a faith that calls out to God in abandonment, and trusts in God even when God's promises don't feel true.

This side of eternity, God will seem to let you down. And even if you know *that's not the real truth*, it will *feel* like the real truth at times.

You don't have to run to the eternal every time your Friday is an abject failure. Even when it feels like God has retreated from your regular week to sit on a distant throne outside of time and beyond suffering, you have the image of Jesus on the cross, abandoned in real time and yet trusting in real time, too.

Sunday's coming; but right now, Friday's here. There is hope for the future; and even in the present, the Spirit is shaping the prayers of Jesus in you. "My God, my God, why have you abandoned me?" "Father, into your hands I commend my spirit."

There is more to the story. But for Good Friday, that's enough.

18. I've Got You Surrounded!

By Justin Rossow

In Philippians 4:4–7, Paul is landing the plane on his letter to these dear friends with some final words of exhortation and encouragement. Verse 7 includes a striking image that holds these verses together: **Paul says that the "peace of God" is actually going to garrison, or guard by placing a sentinel, the hearts and minds of these Philippian believers.**

Since Philippi was a Roman colony, Paul's audience would have had regular, personal experience with a military garrison. A garrison is the place where the soldiers who are not currently on duty are able to rest secure, knowing that a guard has been placed and someone is keeping watch. It is not difficult to image that the people who heard Paul's letter read out loud would have seen Roman sentinels patrolling the borders or the Roman garrison, providing both defense and an early warning system. The result of that military security would have been soldiers well-rested and ready for action.

For Paul, it's the peace of God, not the Peace of Rome, which provides this kind of confident rest and ready preparedness. While the Epistle to the Philippians is a joyful and encouraging letter, you can also tell that the Philippians face real threats, both foreign and domestic.

Paul repeatedly calls for unity in the face of the division that has crept into the Philippian church. Fear for Paul (because he is in jail) and worry about their own financial future seem to be causing some divided hearts and minds; indeed, the word Paul uses for *anxiety* in verse 6 has to do with being divided, or going to pieces.

The way Paul phrases his command not to worry probably indicates that the Philippians are *actively engaged* in that kind of splitting anxiety, and they should stop and desist. Concern for individual status or rights, worry about money, leaders who are divided—all of these seem to be perceived threats to the well-being of the Philippian community.

Paul's remedy for anxiety and division is the peace of God that places a sentinel and patrols the perimeter of the hearts and thoughts of the Philippian church. They can rest from their worry. They can stop being afraid. They can find unity in the midst of division. **Even though they have real reasons to fear, the peace of God that transcends all other reasons now guards, patrols, and garrisons their hearts and minds.**

Paul's answer to anxiety echoes Jesus' teaching on anxiety: worry's opposite and antidote is trusting prayer (see Matthew 6, for example). No perceived threat, big or small, is outside the domain of prayer. In all things, in every situation, thankful prayers bring our needs to God (Phil 4:6), who in turn, stations peace to watch as sentinel over our anxious thoughts and feelings (4:7).

> Do not be anxious about anything, but in everything by prayer and supplication with thanksgiving let your requests be made known to God. And the peace of God, which surpasses all understanding, will guard your hearts and your minds in Christ Jesus.
>
> *Philippians 4:6-7 (ESV)*

The trust evident in such constant prayer is grounded in the close proximity of the coming Christ (Phil 4:5) and the confident joy in the Lord that transcends and permeates your present circumstances (4:4).

> Rejoice in the Lord always; again I will say, rejoice. Let your reasonableness be known to everyone. The Lord is at hand.

> *Philippians 4:4-5 (ESV)*

In these short verses, Paul vividly paints the picture of a community surrounded by the presence and provision of God, grounded in joy and trust, and guarded by peace. What a beautiful way to imagine the Christian Church and our life together as those who belong to the Jesus who is both near to us, and coming soon!

Our congregations and families and friendships face legitimate threats, both internally and externally. Our own preoccupation with individual rights, our worry about family or church budgets, and the evident division between our own leaders—these things cause real uncertainty even for faithful Christians. Your own health, financial upheaval, or family tension can add layers of anxiety and stress.

But the confident joy Paul has in mind doesn't come from removing all potential threats. **For Paul, confidence and joy come from the work of God to surround us and protect us, even as our heavenly Father hears, knows, and provides for our needs.**

Paul invites the Philippian believers, and us along with them, to constant and trusting prayer, prayer grounded in the peace that goes beyond our reasoning—and beyond the legitimate reasons we have to be anxious.

Paul says that peace, the peace that surpasses understanding, surrounds our hearts and minds in Christ Jesus; garrisons our troubled spirits; sets sentinels for fragile hearts.

With all that's going on around you this Advent and Christmas season—all the threats to your personal and family stability, real and imagined—know this: **God's got you surrounded (in a good way!); you have nothing to fear.** Your heart and mind can be at rest. Jesus is near, hears your prayers, and gives you great joy.

FAMILY FOLLOWING

Faith begins at home. It also grows, and expands, gets fueled (and challenged), and practiced (and neglected) at home. If we follow Jesus better when we follow him together, then we also follow Jesus better with the people we are around the most.

Following Jesus with your family isn't always easy. In fact, some of your greatest failures as well as your greatest joys will come in interactions with people you share a table, a TV, and a bathroom with.

Jesus invades your family spaces with refreshing grace and a standing invitation to try again. It's not easy to follow Jesus with your family; but it sure is good, because Jesus is good. If you watch for it, you might find Jesus at work, even in your family.

19. Raising Daughters

By Heidi Goehmann

I was recently asked a question by a friend about raising girls, about raising women: How is it done? Which led to other questions: What's the "right" way? *Is* there a "right" way?

Where do you guide and where do you determine boundaries? How do you teach them to be strong and independent, but also vulnerable, stepping softly when it's needed? How do you help them embrace who God made them to be, and also prepared to deal with all the world will throw at them?

I get to spend my life with two beautiful women who call me "Mom." I am their mentor. I am their FAQ source. I am often their chef; sometimes, their sous chef.

I am their tissue box at times. I am their cheerleader. I am their most opinionated friend. I am their role model. I am their boss at times.

Being a mom to daughters is complicated, much, in the same way, being anything to anyone is complicated. I find it's best when we don't oversimplify the joys and challenges of being a mom. It's also best when we don't oversimplify the joys and challenges in being a daughter.

The joys and challenges can easily become the substance of the thing, but we are here for more. We are here for the relationship.

I get to know these two. I get to find out who they are each day. I get to uncover, like a detective, their strengths, their weaknesses, their hearts, and their amazing minds. That's a huge gift.

As a therapist and a writer, I want parents to be able to embrace *relationship* more, and *moments* a little less. I find this is especially important with my daughters.

Parents have the privilege of knowing deeply these humans who are their children. But my girls aren't *my* girls. They are their own strong, independent girls and women.

It's helpful in any of our relationships to loosen our hands a bit, and remember they rest in God's hands. We get to love them, occasionally we get to teach them, but mostly, our job here is to discover them.

20. Little Helpers

By Kim Longden

Last month, I came across a photo taken over ten years ago that made me smile. I had just finished making Christmas cookies with my kids (all ages five and under at the time) and had snapped a picture of our finished product: odd-shaped, funny-colored, unevenly-sprinkled Christmas cookies adorned the counter.

Although the memory is endearing to me now, I remember feeling frustrated at the time over the fact that having little helpers in the kitchen meant letting go of any hope of perfectly decorated Christmas cookies (or a perfectly decorated Christmas tree, or a perfectly clean house, or perfect *anything* really!).

Little kids are so eager to help, and ten-years-ago me knew that it was good in the long run to let them. However, I hadn't experienced enough of the long run to have a real great perspective on the situation. **Letting my children help was hard for me because it meant letting go of control.** Their "help" made things take twice as long, get twice as messy, and the end result … well … my circus-looking Christmas cookies said it all.

Those intense, early years of parenting began my (still ongoing) process of letting go of things that I thought were important (like perfectly decorated cookies), and exchanging them (in faith) for a greater good that I couldn't see yet. Part of this process involved learning that, even though I didn't need my little kids' "help" to get the job done, letting them participate was about something more important: **deepening our relationship through closeness in time spent together.**

Ten years further up the road of parenting and the process of letting go, I can see how beautiful the cookies in my picture are because I have gained a better perspective of what letting little helpers participate is really about. Taking time to give up on a smooth process or a perfect result has yielded a greater harvest of stronger relationships and treasured memories—which, I have learned, are more important than perfect Christmas cookies, or a perfect house, or a perfect *anything*.

My experience with little helpers gives me new insight into my relationship with my Heavenly Father. The Spirit invites and enables me to participate in God's work in the world, but God doesn't *need* my "help" to accomplish divine purposes. In fact, I've often thought of what a mess I sometimes make when trying to tell someone about Jesus, or awkwardly attempting some act of kindness.

When God lets me participate in the divine work of loving my neighbors or teaching my kids to love Jesus, God is looking for something more important than a smooth process or an efficient result. As I look for what Jesus is doing around me, and then prayerfully ask if I can be part of that, too, the Spirit is deepening our relationship through closeness in time spent together.

My kids are always eager to "help" in the kitchen. So why aren't I as eager to roll up my sleeves and engage the work of the Spirit in my life or in the lives of people around me? Maybe it comes down to the same obstacle I faced when letting my little helpers into the kitchen: **I have an ideal of a perfect result, and I don't like to lose control.**

But if I'm going to act on Jesus' invitation to participate in His mission and His work in the world, I'll need to let go of my idea of what that's supposed to look like, and let the Spirit be in charge of *the process* as well as *the result*.

I don't like letting someone else be in charge. But the lesson I learned from my little helpers makes me think it's worth the risk. My "help" might make things take twice as long and get twice as messy for the Spirit, but engaging with what Jesus is doing in me and around me is about something more important: deepening my relationship with Jesus through closeness in time spent together.

As I look ahead to following Jesus in this year, I want to take the time to give up on a smooth spiritual process or a perfect discipleship result. I'll try letting go of control more often, because I'm longing for a greater harvest of a stronger relationship with Jesus. I'm looking for treasured memories of the Spirit's gentle presence and invitation as I try to see and "help" with what God is doing in my world.

If I can gladly welcome my imperfect little helpers into my kitchen for the sake of building our relationship, how much more will my Heavenly Father invite and empower my imperfect contributions to God's saving activity in the world?

God doesn't need my help; but God wants a deeper relationship with me. The pressure is off: I don't have to control the situation or the outcome. I can just participate with the confidence that the Holy Spirit is at work. What a relief!

21. Star Day!

By Katie Helmreich

I mailed my sister some star-shaped post-it notes this week. A package with a shiny star garland will arrive at her house tomorrow! My brother-in-law is out of town for two weeks and she's on her own with their four little kids. I can't lighten her load much long distance, but I wanted to help them get ready to celebrate Star Day!

Have you ever celebrated Star Day? It's a holiday we made up several years ago. My husband Ben used to travel overseas a lot for work. He'd be gone around two weeks at a time, but total time away in a year was sometimes as much as three or four months.

With a lump in my throat, I'd mark each upcoming trip on the calendar: a doodle of a jet on departure day and **a giant star on the day he'd be back.** The kids and I visited the calendar often counting down, one day at a time, to Star Day!

I stayed home with Elise and Noah, who were toddlers and preschoolers through most of that phase. Man, those days were long... But even in the midst of it (well, maybe a few days after Star Day), it was easy to see God working for good in our family.

We did projects together at the kitchen table and spent quiet hours at the library and Children's Museum. We set up elaborate forts and sometimes ate silly things for meals. We discovered that baths have magical attitude-changing power, especially ones with bath paint, foam ice bergs and arctic animals, or glow sticks!

Talking to my mom on the phone became a daily lifeline. I took the kids down to visit my parents a lot more than we normally would have. Sharing a laugh or an eye roll with another adult was like water to a wilted lettuce. And those late-night conversations with my Dad are precious memories.

To combat particularly bleak days, we made star cookies, star paintings, star garlands, and star Play-Doh ornaments. The kids each had a special Star Day shirt to wear, which we kept on the top of their dresser in anticipation. We papered the living room with star post-it notes. **Constellations of hope!**

Gradually, I learned to take one day at a time, knowing God was always in it with us. By the grace of God, we did what we could. We rejoiced in blessings, embraced encouragement, and we cried when we needed to.

Sometimes it seemed like we'd never make it to Star Day, but we always did! Star Day celebrations meant star-shaped foods, dancing, and tickle fights, usually around Daddy (who had fallen into a jet-lagged coma on the living room floor).

Some Star Days were shinier than others. Our worst was when we were late meeting Ben's flight because we'd been stuck at Urgent Care with a case of pink eye and four ear infections between the three of us.

My favorite Star Day was when we dragged Ben from the airport directly to a hot air balloon lighting festival! Every Star Day was a victory of sorts, a testament to God's mercy and love for us.

Ben changed departments several years back. The calendar has fewer jets on it, and there aren't as many Star Days. The kids think of them with nostalgia, remembering the time we spent celebrating being together again, feeling complete and connected.

My feelings are more mixed. I remember the gut-wrenching days *before* Star Day too clearly. But I also remember all the ways The Creator of the Stars held us safely in His hands.

It's funny: I thought I'd have a bunch of great advice to give my sister after having lived through so many trips myself! But I don't.

Every family, every stage, every situation, every trip is so different. The only constant is Jesus.

My son made up a song that still gets stuck in my head eight years later: "The daytime is nighttime in China! In China the nighttime is day!"

Isn't it incredible that the God who flawlessly manages daytime and nighttime, in China and elsewhere, also comes to us?

Questionably balanced meals, running late for school drop off, pink eye, stomach flu, nasty tempers, no-nappers, frizzy hair, dirty floors, even a stomach full of hot resentment ... nothing. NOTHING keeps Him away.

I wish I could spare my sister and her family the heartaches and hard knocks that come in those days when Daddy's not home. But she's getting through it OK so far! The same God who pulled us through so many times is with her; Jesus is still present with all of God's dearly loved children.

Celebrate all that the Spirit is doing. See the growth God is granting through the challenges today, and look forward with joy to the blessings that will be unveiled tomorrow. Jesus has promised to return: **Star Day is coming!**

22. Be Mine

By Alli Bauck

Fear not, for I have redeemed you;
I have called you by name, you are Mine.

Isaiah 43:1b (ESV)

For the past seven months I've been carrying around an extra weight of worry, all because a white plastic stick revealed some unexpected news: I was pregnant. Normally, this result would have been met with excitement; however, "my plan" for 2022 did not include welcoming a third child into the world.

In different circumstances, I have received that news as a joyful gift. But this time around, it felt more like a burden I reluctantly accepted. And that's how fear became an unnecessary yet unshakable presence in my life.

My fear has taken on many forms: being stressed about an "unplanned" pregnancy, feeling afraid of miscarrying, fearing the loss of friendships due to my prenatal successes and others' fertility failures, uncertainty of how I will manage being a mother of three little boys, and an irrational anxiety that this baby could come earlier than expected.

In my brokenness, I've felt guilt and shame, numbness and denial. I've faked smiles and prayed for peace. I try daily to delight in the precious life growing inside of me, but the devil discerns my doubts and constantly calls my name, luring me away from following God's will. That old snake, in his pride, still thinks that I could belong to him.

But many years ago, a bloody cruciform revealed some unexpected news: I am redeemed. Regardless of all my weaknesses and fears, God chose me and called me by name. The Father bought me back with the precious life of the Beloved Son. The Spirit now equips me for all my vocations, including the calling of a mother.

I know this.

I believe this.

Yet fear still sneaks in.

I think being apprehensive about admitting we are struggling can be part of the snare the devil sets for us, especially since there's always someone we know who is walking through a worse season. So the temptation is to keep quiet about my fears; afraid of confessing how I am feeling at the risk of being judged by others.

But each occasion I've opened up to a family member or friend, their reactions were not ones of criticism. When I admitted my anxieties, they offered reassurance and reminders of my blessings.

I also find hope and encouragement when I turn to God's Word or to prayer. There are countless instances in the Bible that God reminds us to "fear not." In prayerful conversation, Jesus affirms who I am as the Father's beloved child. This brings to mind the words from the Prophet Isaiah 43:1—which also happens to be the verse I chose when I was confirmed: *Fear not, for I have redeemed you; I have called you by name, you are Mine.*

During times of uncertainty, I have people in whom I can confide, and faith resources that reaffirm essential truths. Another outlet that improves my mental health is writing. Sometimes this practice benefits my spiritual health, as well.

On the most recent occasion, I exercised some creativity while trying to express my conflicting feelings as my son's due date draws nearer. I meditated on Isaiah 43 as I thought about how fleeting my fears are when viewed through the lens of God's masterful design.

Even though I can't see beyond my belly (literally: I can't see my feet), I can trust the Father's plan more than my own.

The following poem came from my creative process:

Be Mine
(for Samuel)

I am anxious
to know you
to call you by name
and fall in love with
someone so small
when I first saw
the test result
I was not positive there was
a place in my plans
for you
on a screen I've seen
a black and white blur
with a strong heart
beating in the same body
as mine
with each kick and "hic"
you inform me that
soon
you will need more
than a warm womb
my hands know
how to hold you but
will my head and my heart
be open-armed?
"I am not ready..."
is a silly thing to think because
before the Beginning
you have
already
been
mine.

23. ADVENTURE!

By Katie Helmreich

My daughter, Elise, just turned 13. It's a big deal. So we decided to celebrate with a big adventure! Elise and I headed North for a two-day canoe camping trip. We've done a fair amount of kayaking and a bit of rustic camping, but this was definitely a new experience for both of us. The weather looked great and the calendar was open, so we went for it!

We loaded our supplies into the canoe, let go of the dock, and were swept into our adventure! As the current rushed us along toward the first fallen tree, I suddenly realized that, in our family, I'm not the one who usually steers...

It was exciting though! Like a game really, zipping around each zig and zag and racing to figure out how to navigate the next obstacles as they popped up.

We'd done our research, but somehow I didn't expect the river to be quite so narrow or to have so many blind curves. We'd been told of places we could pull off and get out every half hour or so, but we only saw maybe a quarter of them? Still, we were having a great time, the sun was shining, and we were in it together!

Once I had to hop out of the canoe to push us off a bunch of logs and managed to jump back in again without tipping us over! Another time we skewered ourselves on an innocent looking stick in the middle of the river. We weren't getting anywhere... until a kayaker accidentally ran into us and knocked us clear! She seemed terrified, but we appreciated it. (And no one fell in.)

Just as we were really starting to feel like we were getting the hang of things the wind picked up. It'd been breezy all along, but all of the sudden the wind cranked up to 18-20 mph with 30-40 mph gusts. In a tall ship, on the open main, that probably would have been amazing! In a canoe, on a narrow, winding river with a strong current and lots of fallen trees and debris? Not amazing.

The trees thrashed and creaked on the shore around us. Limbs splintered and cracked, and we could hear several actually falling to the forest floor as we paddled on. What else could we do? There was nowhere to stop, and even when we spotted a place, the current rushed us past it before we could get to the side. If I set down my paddle for even a second, we headed right for the next disaster! It was a white knuckle ride without a moment to grab a drink of water, or even rub the grit out of our eyes.

We struggled on, the current carrying us one way, the wind shoving us another, until we shot around a hairpin bend. A large pile up blocked us on the right, and we managed to veer left in time to miss it. But we couldn't turn back fast enough to avoid the fallen pine that nearly crossed the entire width of the river.

We managed to get Elise past the worst of the branches, but my end of the canoe got sucked right under the middle of the tree. I leaned way over backwards, trying to climb my way out from under it, gripping with my knees, while the current fought to tug the canoe out from under me. It was terrifying.

Elise snatched my paddle as it sped past her, and somehow we got free with only scratches and a boat full of twigs and spiders. The realization that our adventure could have taken a very different turn didn't escape me. But Elise had been badly scared, and it wouldn't help anything for her to know I was freaked out, too.

We had a good long post-trauma laugh together. And we kept going.

I never expected to spend so much of our adventure fervently praying in the back of the canoe: *Please, Lord, this was supposed to be fun! Happy Birthday, Elise! Welcome to life's adventures! Eesh... Please, pleeeeease, just let the wind die down a bit. Please keep us safe! Please help us get off this river! I just wanted Elise to get a taste for conquering challenges, not get walloped by them. Please... Just. Calm. The. Wind. Could you help us figure out where we are? Could you let us find a place to rest for a minute?*

The wind kept howling; getting worse, if anything. The current was relentless. And there were no signs, no fellow boaters, no landings in sight. But we did get to rest whenever we crashed. So... there's that.

We got pretty good at choosing the right logs to crash into! We learned how to turn parallel to them so we could take turns hanging on while the other grabbed a drink or a quick handful of Peanut M&Ms. A few times we crashed into debris on purpose to slow ourselves down, inching our way past, hand over hand, to avoid a worse obstacle.

Please, Lord. We've had enough... I'm not sure why we thought we could do this, but we can't. We're done. Please, just let us spot a landing soon so we can call and have someone pick us up.

After what felt like ages, we passed under the bridge that marked the landing we hoped to use to quit early. We kept our eyes peeled, ready to steer for the bank as soon as we spotted it! But another boat was already there, and before we knew it, we were too far past to have a hope of getting out.

Lord... we just want to quit. Why didn't you let us QUIT?!? What if we can't stop at our campsite either? What if we don't even see it until it's too late? There's no way we'll make it an extra hour and a half to the next campground...

We didn't say much after that. I think we were both just too discouraged... But then we came around yet another bend, and we spotted a canoe up ahead. Somehow knowing we weren't alone helped. We both started paddling harder, finding fresh energy as we worked to keep them in sight!

We managed to maintain the gap for a while, but eventually fell behind. So we crash-rested a minute and noticed that, for the first time in hours, we didn't have to holler at each other to be heard! At some point the wind had begun to die down a bit!

The river gradually got wider and deeper. The current eased a bit. Bliss.

As I was beginning to wonder if maybe we'd already missed our campground, we came up behind three kayakers leisurely floating along. They were discussing camping plans amongst themselves, so we decided to just relax and follow. It was an amazing feeling to let go of that tension after 6 long hours of paddling!

Minutes later, we landed at camp. *Thank you, Lord, for miracles!!*

We set up the tent and enjoyed a hot supper together. I got to know the other couple camping at our campground when our tent door zipper broke beyond repair. They lent me some duct tape. (It didn't actually solve the problem. Oh well.)

I think I was more blessed by the fact that they seemed like normal, nice people to be sharing a piece of wilderness with. It was good for our weary hearts to hear that they'd struggled through similar challenges that afternoon. At one point, they had been frustrated by getting stuck on a pile of logs on a hairpin bend, only to see a large pine tree fall across the river right in front of them!

I didn't like the idea of sleeping in a tent with no door. Who knew what critters would come in and get stuck? But God had already planned for our misadventures! Five or six big, strong trees were places in the perfect places to allow us to feel totally safe. They were the perfect distance apart for our two hammocks. Another allowed us to put up a rainfly in a way that meant we could share, using every inch of our 20' ridgeline cord, like it had been made to order!

Elise snuggled into her sleeping bag, zipped into her bug net cocoon, and was asleep soon. I didn't have a bug net, so I spritzed on a bit more bug spray and wearily climbed into my own hammock.

As I lay there, rocking gently in the light breeze, I watched the lightning bugs dance and the stars glimmer. I picked up my Kindle to read, but discovered the battery had died. Instead, my thoughts drifted back over the day we'd had.

If we hadn't had the delays in leaving the house that morning, we might have seen that tree fall and spent the whole day even more shaken by the experience. If we hadn't learned to embrace crashing, we wouldn't have rested at all! If we'd been allowed to quit, we wouldn't have found this grove of beauty and safety God had prepared for us. If we hadn't come upon the canoe after we missed the landing, we wouldn't have found the strength to take our eyes off the wind and focus on forward.

If we hadn't gotten stuck behind the kayaks, we would have missed the chance to slow down and let go of our frantic energy before arriving at camp. If our tent hadn't broken, we probably wouldn't have talked to the neighbors, and we wouldn't have slept out under the stars.

We set out on an adventure with a plan. Instead, we got an ADVENTURE and had to roll with what God had planned.

I've been worried about facing these teen parenting years. The tween ones weren't exactly all sunshine and daises, and my own teen experience left some scars...

How are we going to manage to get through this next phase together? There are so many ways the experience could be fun and exciting! But what if instead we face 30-40 mph wind gusts and obstacle after obstacle?

Well... we're not heading into them empty handed. We have a canoe full of past experiences and resources. We've done a little research. We've watched and learned from the ways others navigate the current.

The wind may come; the obstacles will be there. But God will give us chances to crash. We'll probably even get better at recovering from disasters as we go. By the power of the Holy Spirit, we'll see them as opportunities to rest, to reconnect, share a snack, and then get right back out into the river.

The Father won't let us quit. But God will keep on sending our brothers and sisters in Christ to paddle the river with us and to keep us motivated to quit looking at the wind and instead look to Jesus.

Our Shepherd will guide us to the places of rest He has prepared for us. He'll even bless us with little miracles (like waking up without a single bug bite after a night out in the open).

The Holy Spirit will continue to work in Elise and help her mature and grow into a beautiful woman of God!

We set out for the final leg of our trip the next morning. The river was still moving swiftly, and the wind was picking up, but overall, it was a much calmer canoeing experience. We had the chance to chat as we paddled to our destination.

After a quiet pause, Elise piped up, "Isn't it amazing how many 'coincidences' God blesses us with? I can't even really count them all, and it's only been 24 hours since we left home!"

Yes! God is good!

"Mom? We should do this again sometime."

24. Christ in the Mouth of My Brother or Sister

By Justin Rossow

Our youngest daughter started high school today. Oof. I remember my dad dropping me off for my first day of high school, so it was an honor to drop my daughter off at the literal crack of dawn this morning.

Of course, she was a little nervous (like I was); and of course, she will be fine. We talked and imagined and even prayed together as we tried to find the best route with the least traffic and discover where to turn and where to drop off.

I got back to my desk and started my busy day the way I now typically do; with 20 minutes of Scripture and prayer. Today I am in John 6, and I like the translation of verse 20 in the version I am using right now. The disciples are caught in a storm and Jesus shows up, trampling the waves, to say, "Don't be afraid. I am here!"

Of course, you could take the original several different ways, including, "Don't be afraid. It is I!" or even, "Stop being afraid! I AM!" But I like the simplicity and the promise of "Don't be afraid. I am here!"

I wished I had read those words before our commute this morning, so I could have shared them with my daughter.

After my time in the Word, I turned to the task I have in front of me today. I'm working on a project about the adventure of "walking with," what it means to say we follow Jesus better when we follow Him together. When I talk about relational discipleship, I like to paraphrase Dietrich Bonhoeffer this way:

> **The Christ in the mouth of my brother or sister is stronger than the Christ in my own heart; my heart is uncertain, the Word is sure.**

I love that sentiment, though I know it's my own version of what Bonhoeffer said, so I always have to go back to the original to make sure I am getting it right. Here's the context and how Bonhoeffer actually puts it in his book, *Life Together:*

> God has put this Word into the mouth of others in order that it may be communicated to us. When one person is struck by the Word, he speaks it to others. God has willed that we should seek and find his living Word in the witness of a brother, in the mouth of a man. Therefore, the Christian needs another Christian who speaks God's Word to him. He needs him again and again when he becomes uncertain and discouraged, for by himself he cannot help himself without belying the truth.
>
> He needs his brother as a bearer and proclaimer of the divine word of salvation. He needs his brother solely because of Jesus Christ.
>
> **The Christ in his own heart is weaker than the Christ in the word of his brother; his own heart is uncertain, his brother's is sure.**

Of course, Bonhoeffer is writing to an all-male seminary community at the time, so it makes sense to update his language a little. But the idea, that God put the divine Word on the lips of ordinary people in my life *so that I can actually receive God's Word of divine promise in my ordinary life* is a profound insight.

We know Jesus is the Word of God from eternity and to eternity. And we know the Scriptures are the Word of God, the faithful message recorded and received, that grounds our faith and proclamation. And the Word of God I hear most often and receive when I need it most comes in, with, and under the words of my friends and family, my wife and children, my pastor and my neighbor.

God puts the divine Word into the human mouths of the humans around me in my everyday life so I can hear and receive God's divine Word in my all-too-human life every day.

But as the Sword of the Spirit, the Word of God cuts both ways, as it were. If God puts the Word into the mouths of real people in my real life for my sake, God also puts the divine Word in my all-too-human mouth for the sake of the people I interact with every day.

My time of solitude with the Word isn't an escape from the world; nor is that time of meditation only for my benefit. I don't go to the Word just to see what Jesus has for me today; I go on behalf of my family and friends, my wife and children, my pastor and my neighbor.

That was the real insight of my time in Scripture this morning: I didn't go there alone, and I didn't receive just for me. I wished I had read those words of promise before I drove my daughter to her first day of high school...

But I have learned that, with Jesus, a "missed opportunity" is usually just a chance to be open to something you weren't expecting.

Maybe Bonhoeffer needs even a little more updating...

Maybe we could say, "God has put this Word onto the Instagram of others in order that it may be communicated to us ...?"

"Every follower of Jesus needs other followers who snapchats the Word of God to them?"

"The Christ in the text of my brother or sister is stronger than the Christ in my own heart ...?"

Whatever, the idea still stands: God's Word is given to specific individuals in your life so that you can hear it from them; and God gives you the Word so that specific individuals in your life can hear it from you, whatever mode or media that takes.

So I took a picture of John 6:20 and texted it to my daughter during her first day of high school. (Yes, even freshmen are allowed phones at school. What is this world coming to??) Along with the picture I sent a brief note: "From my reading this morning. For you, from Jesus."

That pretty much sums up what I learned from Dietrich Bonhoeffer again today. The Word was there for me; but it wasn't just for me. The Word of promise was for my daughter, through me, so that her uncertain heart would receive a sure Word: "Don't be afraid. I am here! Even on your first day of high school!"

25. Peace in the Process

By Kim Longden

A few days ago, I was sitting in the optometrist's office with nine-year-old Jonah listening to the hushed tones of the eye exam in progress: "What is the lowest line you can read? Does it look better through lens number one, or number two?"

It was a quiet and routine dialogue, almost a murmur under the whirring of the air conditioning vents. My only role at that point was to be present, seated in the corner observing. I did not take this peaceful moment for granted. In the not-too-distant past, we would have been struggling big time to get through an appointment like this!

It all began several years ago when we realized that then four-year-old Jonah wasn't seeing well. We made an appointment with the local eye doctor which turned into months of many visits with specialists throughout the state. Not knowing if he was just extremely nearsighted, or if something was wrong with his overall eye health was pretty stressful.

But what made things exponentially more difficult was trying to get an anxious four-year-old to sit still long enough for the examinations that needed to be done. The child who is screaming and thrashing loud enough all the other patients can hear through closed doors? That was him. The mother who everyone is looking at like she can't control her kid? That was me. It was a lengthy process of trying one thing and then another before we started getting insight into what was going on with his vision.

Remembering those stressful, sweaty, tear-filled appointments got me thinking as I sat in my corner of the quiet exam room. When kids are young, their reality is the here and now; and when "here and now" is uncomfortable, they react.

Children don't really have a concept of the big picture, so often our efforts at helping are perceived as confusing, disorienting, and even painful to them. My strong-willed son didn't know that these distressing examinations with stinging eye drops and bright lights shining in his eyes were what he needed to be helped. In fact, Jonah had no idea at the age of four that he needed help. He had no clue he couldn't see well, because he didn't know any different! My little boy just knew the process was painful and uncomfortable and wanted it to end. Now!

I pondered what would've happened if we'd just stopped requiring Jonah to go to his eye appointments because they were difficult for him. This would have been a tempting thought back then; I dreaded those appointments, too. However, my view of the big picture and love for my son would not have allowed me to do that.

No matter how much Jonah resisted, I knew we had to continue walking this path because it was best for him. He had to trust me as we continued each step forward, even though he didn't understand why.

I started to think about how, just like little kids, I often don't have a big picture perspective of pain and suffering in my life. I just know it hurts and I want it to end. Now! The moment hard times come, I want to run away, just like Jonah wanting to flee those exam rooms.

I've had many tearful moments begging God to take away every difficulty. Which makes me wonder: Maybe my Heavenly Father walks with me through struggles for my good, just like I walked with Jonah through his tough eye appointments...? Maybe I can fully trust God with the big picture I cannot see...?

Many times, all Jonah could do was take my hand and step through the doors of those doctors' offices, not knowing what would happen next. Maybe Jesus invites me to do the same: to take a next step in trust with Him, even though I have no idea what awaits.

Just like my son didn't even know he couldn't see, I am likely oblivious to some of the places I need the most help. When I can't see the "why" of suffering in my limited perspective, I can cling to the truth that Jesus is good, and Jesus is for me.

As our peaceful eye appointment ended that day, we received a new referral to another specialist. There has not been a neat and tidy resolution to this journey. We still have unknowns regarding Jonah's eye health. The only difference is that now there is more peace in the process, for Jonah and for me.

Jesus tells us that we will have difficulties in this world. He doesn't promise trouble-free living; He promises peace that transcends human understanding. Peace in the process: the very priceless thing I was marveling over in the exam room.

And so, Jonah and I take the next step forward into the unknown: his little hand in mine, and my hand in my Heavenly Father's firm and trustworthy grasp.

26. School Photos

By Valerie Matyas

Remember picture day at school? Finding the perfect outfit of which only 1/8th will be visible. Practicing a natural smile in the mirror, varying the degree of eye crinkle and teeth exposure. Experimenting with hairstyles while trying to calculate how long fresh curls will hold, or a cowlick will stay tamed.

Ah, picture day! Both exciting and nerve wracking; a moment to capture; a visible reminder of an entire school year. Missing teeth, glasses, braces, pimples, and dimples all laid bare in an 8 x 10 proudly displayed for an entire year. For better or worse, picture day makes memories forever memorable.

Our four kids brought home their school photos last week. All parties involved (both those posing in front of the camera and those footing the bill) were pleased with the results. So off the wall came the four wooden frames to engage in the annual changing of the guard. Out with the old and in with the new.

One by one, the process is the same: before entering the frame the new photo is meticulously hand labeled with the child's first, middle, and last name, his or her grade level, the name of the school, and the hyphenated school year. (This format matches the precise cataloging of the numerous photos that already inhabit the frame.)

Then the entire series of existing photos are arranged on the table in ascending order for their once-a-year moment to be viewed, appraised, and cherished. The ritual is clerical in nature, yet delightfully playful and endearing.

It brings me great joy to see how much each child has grown, how they have changed, and yet remain very much who they were in their youngest image. It is fun to see their likeness to one another and to their close and distant relatives.

So much can change in one year, and yet the day-to-day changes are almost imperceptible. It makes me wonder if spiritual maturity can be noticed day to day, or if it is best perceived from a vantage point spanning many years ...

Our children desire to get taller and stronger. They want to climb higher, run longer, and swim deeper. My husband and I have told them since they were little: eat your vegetables, drink plenty of water, and get a good night's sleep if you want to be strong like dad and mom.

I wonder if we have been as verbally intentional to explain why we as a family attend worship weekly, read Scripture daily, and pray before meals, bed, long road trips, and during tough situations? Do they know those are ways to grow spiritually strong like dad and mom?

I wonder if they understand that spiritual maturity doesn't make you independent and less reliant, but actually more dependent on your Savior, through whom you will see more, serve more, love more, and give more?

School photos are clear evidence that our children grow physically every day, even if the incremental change is sometimes hard to see. I desire their spiritual growth to be as evident over time as their physical growth. I want their spiritual likeness to mature and transform more and more to the image of Jesus. I want them to see the world through His eyes, and eventually, I want the world to see Him in their actions.

My oldest daughter looks quite a bit like me.

My oldest son is a dead ringer for my husband.

My youngest son is the spitting image of my mom's brother, and my youngest daughter is a beautiful combination of several relatives, giving her the unique opportunity to be told, "You look just like your mom," or "Wow, you sure look like your daddy."

Watching them grow and mature is both an honor and a joy.

I catch glimpses of the Spirit at work in their lives, too: a kind word, a gentle action, being quick to forgive or ask for forgiveness.

Some days, it's clear that they have more growing to do, but already now I see a certain family resemblance to the Body of Christ.

My kids point me back to Jesus.

So school photos, likenesses, and images aside, no matter whom they favor physically, I pray that their thoughts, words, and deeds continue to grow to resemble Christ.

27. *Click*

By Katie Helmreich

We're near the finish line! A 1000 piece puzzle, with 360 Lego Minifigure Faces, almost done! Almost.

With this particular puzzle, few of our standard puzzle-solving tricks seem to work. Literally everything is yellow or shadowed yellow. But we've finally got all the faces in!

The pieces we've got left are pretty much all Lego *necks*. We're to that stagnant stage when you've got around thirty pieces left and none of them seem to fit in any of the thirty-ish gaps that are left.

One Lego lady is missing a fair amount of her distinctively blue goggles, and there's no way it's one of these pieces. Maybe it's lost? Time will tell.

One of the pieces has a randomly long strip of white on the edge that absolutely does NOT make sense. I've tried it everywhere. Multiple times. But just now it clicked into place. Crazy!

I'm still not entirely sure how it worked. I even took the piece back out and looked at it again: it still doesn't look like that piece should fit in that opening. But it does!

We're all at home this week, sniffling our way through COVID and quarantine, so I've spent a lot of time working on this puzzle lately. It's not what I had planned for this week, but it's what I have energy for.

Looking at these random, impossible pieces reminds me of times when our plans have fallen apart into chaos.

Last summer the kids and I went down to my parents' house and planned to take a day trip to see my grandma together. A sweet and simple plan! That was derailed almost immediately when the Suburban started growling like a rock tumbler before we'd driven a quarter mile.

We turned around and gingerly encouraged the Suburban back into my parents' driveway. By the time I put it in park it was billowing smoke. (The kids have never leapt out of the vehicle as fast as they did that morning!) Ben, my husband and tele-mechanic, was able to diagnose the issue via video chat. Mom and I eventually figured out a multi-step plan for getting a different vehicle, and we had a precious visit with Grandma after all!

While we were gone, Ben packed up some tools and drove down to handle the issue with the Suburban. It didn't take him long to get it to a point where it was safe to drive home. And since he was already there, Ben tackled a big project my parents were unable to do because of their own, recently derailed plans.

Looking at the pieces individually, none of it makes sense. Some of the pieces didn't even seem to be part of the same puzzle! How does billowing smoke fit into the same picture as plumbing progress? Our schedule was pretty tight at the time; how in the world did all the events of that day fit into the same ten hours?

The day was even more memorably special because it clicked into place so neatly after all had seemed impossible!

There's a lot we do to order our lives. Without a plan, nothing happens. It's a great feeling when things come together and we get a bit of momentum going as the pieces fit together!

At other times, we sit staring at the same thirty-odd Lego Minifigure neck puzzle pieces wondering how this will ever be anything.

Sometimes we're more aware of the fact that our plans are simply within God's plans. God's plans don't often make obvious sense, especially beforehand.

But then … *Click.* The impossible happens again. Unexpected connections are made and relationships formed. Miracles happen.

Sometimes prayers aren't answered the way we'd hoped. Instead, we're blessed with opportunities to see how our hardship helped to prepare us to support others.

The only way to finish the puzzle is to keep trying each piece, one at a time, one gap at a time if need be. It'll come together. The people that made the puzzle wouldn't have thrown in any pieces that aren't part of this picture. (Although it is entirely possible we've lost that one piece with the Lego lady's blue goggles …)

It takes time and persistence. And like a lot of things, it's better when you work with someone else; better still if you work while sharing a good conversation or an audiobook.

What is God doing with that weird piece in your life right now? Not sure. But let's keep on keeping on. The One who made us wouldn't have given us the wrong pieces.

Let's look at it from a different angle, or maybe come back to it later. In the meantime, it's a joy to be working alongside you! Won't it feel awesome when we see how that piece clicks into place?

And if it turns out a piece is actually missing or lost? Well, we know a few good stories that tell of the lengths Jesus will go to find it …

Being Myself, with Jesus

What if Jesus loved you just as you are,
just *who* are you are today, experiencing everything
you are experiencing in your regular, ordinary life?

What if Jesus knew, and cared, all about your
moments and your days—moments and days filled
with ups and downs, joys and sorrows, small victories
and plenty of defeat?

What if you could just be yourself, with Jesus?

28. Noticing My Need for Spiritual Rest

By Alli Bauck

As a stay-at-home-mom with two active boys between the ages of 1 and 4 (and in my second trimester with boy #3), I try to make time for—and not take for granted—physical rest. Naptime and nighttime are sacred at our house.

Maybe that's why a quote from @coolurbanhippie on social media recently caught my attention:

> I don't know who needs to hear this but rest is not a reward.
> You don't have to earn rest. You need rest. You deserve rest.
> You are worthy of rest simply because you are a living being.
> And don't ever feel guilty for taking time to rest.

I was halfway through my daily gratitude journaling for the month of November when I realized that four of the blessings all shared this theme: sleeping in; rest; naps; and a restful night's sleep. Did I mention, I really treasure moments of physical rest?

While I am grateful for physical rest, I have a more difficult time prioritizing moments of spiritual rest. Perhaps it is because I don't see the need for spiritual rest as clearly in my daily life? I'm often too busy to notice when my faith fuel tank symbol lights up. Also, I think Satan prefers it when I'm running on empty. He constantly distracts me from that little warning light because he doesn't want me visiting God's grace station. But God seems to think both physical and spiritual rest are divine gifts intended for our good.

On the seventh day of creation, God rested (Genesis 2:2). Aren't we tempted to view this holy hiatus as a result of God's cosmic construction project? But God is not human; the Almighty doesn't need to take a personal day from being the Ruler of the Universe. God rested on the seventh day to set a gracious example for us and appoint the Sabbath for us to observe each week (Genesis 2:3).

The Sabbath rest can even be called a covenant and sign between God and God's chosen people (Exodus 31:12-17), and a covenant or promise of relationship even foreigners can hold onto (Isaiah 56:1-8). The

Sabbath belongs to the promise that makes God's people unique and a blessing to the world.

The Bible also tells us that Jesus rested. As the Word made flesh, Jesus shared our human likeness and frequently retreated in isolation to recharge for His earthly ministry. In these times of pause, Jesus prayed and slept, experiencing the need and the blessing of physical and spiritual rest. I love the fact that Jesus even took naps!

When I am physically tired, I have some methods for dealing with it (naps being high on my list). But when it comes to spiritual rest and renewal, I find my options and my experience much more limited. Maybe that's why I don't notice when I am spiritually tired as often, and why I am slower to try and refuel when I do notice.

What would be the spiritual equivalent of going to bed early, or setting the alarm an hour later, or taking a power nap? What patterns or activities would allow for refilling my faith fuel tank?

Thinking about spiritual rest as a natural part of a healthy life and looking for habits that help, I notice that I already have some go-to activities that help me take a spiritual siesta.

Reading for Rest

I like reading. Reading refreshes me. Sometimes I will even read to fall asleep, combining two of my favorite blessings: books and naps.

Because I like reading, the right kind of reading can also restore my soul. I like reading the Bible. There is an overwhelming amount of it, though, and it can be dense and sometimes confusing. So I also like reading resources that include Scripture and also show me how the meaning of the words gets applied in real life. This type of devotional reading is a kind of spiritual rest for me.

Recently, I got to be part of a collaborative project from Next Step Press. I was thrilled when my copy of *Be Still and Notice* came in the mail and I got to see my name in print! But then I started reading what other people had contributed. I found people, like me, who often struggle, and who always need Jesus, and who sometimes have profound insight that inspires me to take deep, enlightening breaths.

If you are more of an extrovert, having a meaningful conversation with friends might be an equivalent for you. I enjoy visiting with friends; but I have also found meaningful spiritual renewal by reading.

Creating for Rest

I like to be creative. I enjoy writing, and journaling, and crafting. I like making something with my mind and hands that speaks truth to my eyes and heart. I find, as a creative person, the creative act is a kind of spiritual rest, especially when that creativity is connected to God's Word.

That's one reason I love being part of the *Light in the Darkness* Social Learning group for Advent. The hymn journal the group uses includes faith experiments that let me focus on Scripture in new ways. The music and the devotions and the podcasts for each chapter all feed both my soul and my creative side.

The word "inspiration" is related to the word for "spirit" and the word for "breath". The time spent engaging my whole person feels like a form of spiritual meditation. Although not everything I try turns out the way I hoped, I find being creative with the Spirit is a breath of fresh air in my hectic week!

Learning for Rest

My favorite kind of learning was never limited to the classroom. I enjoy learning how to cook a new recipe or trying fun activities with my kids. I like finding out more about #momlife from people I trust who have been there before.

Even the process of trying, and failing, and getting better at something can be a source of delight. Learning isn't always fun the whole time, but I've noticed how learning something new can refresh me spiritually.

This fall, Visual Faith® Ministry launched a year-long online invitation to spiritual learning called *The Movable Adventure*. I got to be a small part of the big picture. But watching these videos, listening to stories of transformation, learning and trying new ways of engaging God's Word—it's all been a rejuvenating way of staying connected to Jesus.

The videos are short, but there are lots of them, so I get to pick what interests me today. Maybe that's part of the key to Learning for Rest: choosing something to learn that's relevant and interesting to you right now. In any case, I've found that time in The Movable Adventure has helped me feel well-rested spiritually.

What are some ways you practice rest in your life? Do you take power naps? Or sleep in on your day off?

How do you rest spiritually? Do you Read for Rest, Create for Rest, or Learn for Rest? Or do you have other tools or methods that help you fill up your spiritual fuel tank?

Noticing what helps you rejuvenate your faith life might even help you notice when you need to refuel, and give you a plan for what to do when you just need to rest and refresh your soul.

It's OK to be tired, physically and spiritually. Rest is not a reward for working hard; rest is a basic human need, hard-wired by God and modeled by Jesus. In your pauses for rest, you get to practice dependence on the grace and power of God, Who renews all things.

Whew! I'm going to go take a nap...

29. Remembering Things that Make You Smile

By Justin Rossow

I have been reading a book lately by Chris M. Coursey called *The Joy Switch: How Your Brain's Secret Circuit Affects Your Relationships— and How You Can Activate It*. Yes, it's about as cheesy as it sounds. BUT the author is actually taking relatively recent brain science and dumbing it down so we can understand it and apply it to our lives of faith. Speaking neuroscience to lay people ends up sounding kind of cheesy sometimes; it's an occupational hazard.

So cheese notwithstanding, I've found some helpful stuff in this book. One of the suggested activities, based on brain science, has to do with remembering things that make you smile. You could paraphrase the basics in three steps:

1. Remember.
2. Feel.
3. Share.

First, you **Remember**. Remember something that makes you smile. It could be a person, a place, an activity, or even a certain food.

This time of year, I remember the dozens of different kinds of Christmas cookies my grandma used to bake, from cornflakes Christmas wreaths, to chocolate-covered Chow Mein bird's nests, to pastel-colored marshmallow stained glass windows rolled in chopped pecans. Remembering grandma and her glorious display of cookies makes me smile.

Second, you **Feel**. You feel the feelings the memory brings. You allow yourself to experience again that experience that brought you joy. Coursey suggests you should think about *where you remember that experience in your body* as a way of recalling the experience more fully.

For me, I hold the memory of grandma's mountains of cookies in my eyes (which always opened wide at the display) and in my lips, teeth, and tongue (not only because of the wonderful taste, but because of all the amazing textures of crunchy, gooey, melty, or powdery that poked or oozed or coated the roof of my mouth).

Remembering something that makes you smile and recalling that experience in your body goes a long way to helping you feel appreciation. But that sense of gratefulness is taken to another level when you include step 3: you **Share**. Share a simple story about that memory with another person. Talk about why it makes you smile and where it lives in your body, and your brain and body begin to respond as if you were actually living out that joyful moment right now.

The appreciation you feel for that moment of joy, in brain science terms, **increases neuronal density in the ventromedial and ventrolateral prefrontal cortex**. In less technical (but more cheesy) terms, the relationship circuit in your brain turns on. You are more open to other people and what is going on in their lives right now. You are more emotionally and intellectually available, more likely to be happy, and a lot easier to get along with.

When you feel appreciation and joy, you begin to look for more things that make you feel appreciation and joy. It's an upward spiral that gets easier with practice. **The more you remember, feel, and share something that makes you smile, the easier it is for you to notice, experience, and remember something that makes you smile.**

I think following Jesus is like that.

The more you joyfully remember something Jesus did in your life that makes you smile, the more often you share simple experiences of Jesus in your regular life, the easier it is for you to notice, experience, and remember what Jesus is doing in you or around you.

Of course, not everything is easy or light in your experience of faith. But seeing and remembering Jesus active even in the midst of your grief, or your struggle, or your sin can still be a memory that brings a sense of appreciation, and gratitude, and even joy.

So this Christmas, I'll be remembering grandma's homemade, melt-in-your-mouth fudge squares and her almond crescents that always left a trail of white powdered sugar down the front of your sweater.

But I'll also be remembering the time Jesus showed up in a difficult conversation with my daughter and turned it into prayer; the time the Spirit invited and motivated me to travel to a strange place where strange people were eating strange foods (it was across the street) and simply be a person of peace in the midst of a foreign birthday party; or the time God's Word reminded me clearly and specifically how much my Heavenly Father loves me, and delights in me, and rejoices over me with singing.

Those moments put a smile on my face and help me find a sense of appreciation for what Jesus has been doing in my life. **But remembering, and feeling, and sharing those moments also teaches me to look for more of the same: times when Jesus shows up in my ordinary life in faithful and gracious ways.**

So the next time you get together with friends or family, I invite you to practice a little brain science. **Remember** something that makes you smile. **Feel** those feelings again and recall where that experience lives in your body's memory. Then **share** that experience with someone else. We follow Jesus better when we follow him together.

30. My Christmas Letter to God

By Alli Bauck

Every year, right after Thanksgiving I debate sending a family Christmas card. In previous years I have justified my participation in this holiday tradition because we had recently updated our family photos or we had some life-changing event occur. Other years, I have nothing "exciting" to share or I feel like it's just "one more thing" filling my festive plate.

However, I think the real reason I feel compelled to write a family letter is the process. December is the last month of the calendar—the perfect time to reflect on all the happenings of that year. As I synopsize the highlights from the past eleven months of our existence, I start to see the whole picture.

Being a creative person, I like challenging myself to think outside the box. I don't want my letter to come off as braggy or to read like a news report. This year, as I sat staring at a blank page in my notebook, I began to wonder: does anyone really care? Besides the handful of family and friends who look forward to our Christmas card—is it just a waste of time and money, a dying tradition?

And then I thought I heard a voice saying, "Alli, I want you to share your story with Me. Write Me a Christmas letter." Writing a letter to God seemed like an awkward undertaking, but I decided to take the Spirit up on this request.

If I were to address my Christmas letter to the Almighty, maybe it would go something like this:

Dear Heavenly Father,

As another calendar year concludes, I'm taking a moment to reflect on the joys (and struggles) of 2021. Your faithfulness to my family can be seen in the scribbles on our planner pages, like March 9th when William turned three, or September 4th when Levi became a one-year-old (and we were able to celebrate with both sides of our family).

On Sunday, May 30th, the word "Church" was written down for the first time in a year; You allowed us to return to in-person worship with our family of faith. Recently, Jason and I marveled at how our marriage has evolved as we marked our 10th anniversary. For all these milestones, I praise and thank You!

During the weekdays, Your hand of provision was evident as we walked in our vocations. I am grateful that Jason was able to work remotely this year and I could be at home with the boys.

Gradually, our weekend visits with family resumed, and we remembered to reserve some weekends for rest. Even on the days not marked by memorable moments, You continued to provide us with abundant blessings. On the days we can't remember (or wish we could forget), Your grace embraced us, from sunrise to sunset.

Personally, the year 2021 will be significant because of all the doors I witnessed You open for me. I did not seek out opportunities to share my spiritual gifts; but You kept encouraging me to step outside my comfort zone. In March, I was a co-presenter for the first ever Visual Faith™ Ministry virtual retreat; and again I was asked to share my story as part of the VFM Movable Adventure that launched in November. I contributed to a women's devotional book that will be available through Concordia Publishing House (2022), and my name appears alongside other inspirational followers of Jesus in the second annual anthology from the Next Step Community.

But the most challenging change You designed for us this year was revealed when I witnessed what looked like a black and white gummy bear wiggling on a screen, in the ultrasound room of the women's clinic.

Of all the things planned (and unplanned), this new addition to our lives realigned my will with Yours. I quickly realized that my human nature was preventing me from embracing the joy of welcoming another child into our hearts.
When my focus shifted from "my plan" to trusting in Your perfect one, I began to feel at peace with the precious life tumbling around in my tummy.

I cannot predict what this next year will bring but I pray that Your will—above and beyond mine—would be done. I hope that 2022 is the year Jesus returns in glory to finish what began in a Garden, was fulfilled at Christmas, culminated on the Cross, and was restored on Easter.

While we wait and look for that final consummation, help me receive each day as a gift and grant me strength to live out Your story in my life.

Joyfully Yours,

Alli

31. Walking in the Light

By Kristeen Bruun

I am in love with God again. It won't last, I know that. It never does. But for now, I am enjoying walking light upon the earth, smiling the secret smile of lovers, taking delight in the gifts I am given. The gifts are always there. But I don't always have the awareness that being in love brings to them.

Possibly this state of being in love came about because I lived through several very intense experiences in a short span of time.

It began with an unusually powerful Christmas sermon. The state of our world had dumped me into a depression. Not just COVID, which has brought so much death and suffering (and which isn't finished yet), but our own inability to make any except selfish choices, thus creating even more suffering.

Then my pastor preached a sermon on Christ our light and on the promise that, no matter what happens, the light cannot be extinguished. He was brave enough to specify some of the forces of darkness that seem to surround us, but to emphasize that, even so, the light *cannot* be extinguished.

I felt a glimmer of hope. I went from that sermon to a week with family. I have spent many Christmas weeks with family in my life, some good, some not so good, and some leading to even more depression. But never have I spent a week like this one, in which I was so bathed in love.

It hit me hard, coming off the Christmas sermon, realizing that here was light. Not a great light. Not a light to transform the world, perhaps. But enough light to keep the five of us going into the new year.

After the calendar changed, I went to work. (I am semi-retired, or as one of my friends tells me, I failed retirement.) I work two months, January and August, the two months that start the spring and fall semesters, at my old job in the college bookstore.

The money's helpful. The collegiality is uplifting. I appreciate the teamwork. Together we get through the rush.

This year was different. The servers that power our cash registers went down for most functions, and the manager, for whom I work, was called away because of a death in the family, both during the first week of school. So corporate sent in a substitute manager.

Now, normally, I think that, "I'm from corporate, and I'm here to help you," qualifies as one of the world's top jokes, along with "The check's in the mail." But this woman was different.

While working to solve our server problem, she also created work-arounds that kept us up and running. She got the best out of us without trying to turn us into some other store. It was an honor to work long hours as her assistant.

At the same time, I was journeying with the manager, Carleton, a friend of mine, and with his family as they said their good-byes to their husband and father and planned a funeral. I sing in the choir with Carleton's mother and sister, and the choir sang for the funeral.

I texted more during that week than I have at any time since I owned my phone. I also spent a lot of time in prayer for my friend and his family.

I felt as if I were living two lives, both incredibly intense.

"See," said God, "for this I put you on the planet.

"For this I sent you all of your life experiences, so that you would be prepared to offer your support this week in several ways.

"Look, just look, at all the light I've been sending you, so that you could share it!"

"I get it," I said.

OK; what I mean is, "I get it *now*."

I will probably forget and need reminding.

I feel like Mary when she sang the Magnificat. "My soul magnifies the Lord, and my spirit rejoices in God my savior, for he has looked on the humble estate of his servant" (Luke 1:47-48).

God has given me gifts that fill me with light, and called me to tasks that allow me to share the light.

For now, I walk in the light of his love.

32. Getting to the Heart of the Matter

By Justin Rossow

I recently heard my good friends Steve and Jamie from Breathe Life Ministries lead a presentation on noticing yourself with God. As part of that workshop, they talked about how the biblical understanding of the "heart" is a little more complex than how we use the term in English.

Not only is the "heart" the seat of your conscience (Hebrews 10:22), the New Testament uses "heart" where we might typically use other words or locations. For example, in our culture we might say your thoughts exist in your mind; Matthew 9:4 talks about thoughts in your heart. We might say your resolute purpose resides in your will; Acts 11:23 speaks of a resolute purpose in your heart. You can find other examples, but the main idea is that for at least some of the cultures represented by the library of writings we call The Bible, **the heart is a more diverse place than we typically make it out to be.**

It's not that emotions don't belong in your heart in biblical usage—sorrow, for example, fills the hearts of the disciples in John 16:22. But **your heart is the primary organ of *feeling* in our culture; in the biblical text, the heart seems to be much, much more.**

In my Scripture reading this morning I was in Mark 6, right after the Feeding of the 5,000. The disciples in a boat at night, rowing hard against the wind (and Jesus sees them—take comfort! Jesus sees you!). As the reading winds down, Mark says the disciples "didn't **understand** about the loaves because their **hearts** were hard." That puts the seat of **understanding** in the **heart.**

That reminded me of how the LORD grants Solomon's request in 1 Kings 3:12 by giving the king a wise and understanding ... well, *heart* in the NIV, but *mind* in the ESV: the Hebrew word is *lev;* look it up in your Hebrew dictionary and *lev* **(rhymes with brave) refers to the inner person, the mind, will, or heart.**

So, the CENTER of a person...? I think that might be right.

Maybe the HEART of a person, biblically speaking, is connected to the CENTER of the person, and therefore the most important, most central, most true or prototypical of that person.

Our brains work with concepts and categories in a way that places the most important or representative thing in the center of the category and less typical, less important, less representative examples on the periphery of the concept. So a robin, for example, is at the center of our concept BIRD, while a penguin or ostrich would be still in the category, but much farther away from the center; somewhere on the periphery.

This distinction between CENTER and PERIPHERY is hardwired into our cognitive system by the way our human brains work in our human bodies. (I won't go into that more right now, but you don't have to take my word for it. Check out books like *Surfaces and Essences: Analogy as the Fuel and Fire of Thinking*; or *Philosophy in the Flesh: The Embodied Mind and its Challenge to Western Thought*; or, my personal favorite, *Women, Fire, and Dangerous Things: What Categories Reveal About the Mind*.)

After hearing Steve and Jamie talk about the heart, and reflecting on what I have learned about the cultures and languages of the Bible, and about cognitive linguistics, **my new working theory is that the concept of the HEART in the Bible is directly related to what belongs at the CENTER of a person, as opposed to the PERIPHERY.** That certainly could include emotions, but not *all* emotions; and not *only* emotions.

In English, we can refer to "the heart of the matter," and by that we mean the most central, important, and essential elements at stake (not, for example, just the emotions related to the topic). But by and large, **we tend to reserve the heart for emotions, and emotions for the heart.**

The heart isn't the only organ of emotion in the Bible. The intestines or GUTS can house strong emotion, like compassion (in Matthew 15:32, for example, Jesus has compassion, literally, his *guts* twisted, in Greek, *splagchnizomai*, for the crowd). English also has phrases like "gut-wrenching," but I think, linguistically and conceptually, we prefer the *heart* as the seat of *emotion*; and we oppose *the heart* to *the brain* as the seat of *thought*. **Heart = emotion; brain = thought.**

But that basic duality is not typical of the Bible. At the beginning of Matthew 15, for example, some Pharisees ask Jesus about hand-washing rules. In response, Jesus calls them hypocrites and quotes Isaiah 29:

> These people honor me with their ***lips***,
>> but their **hearts** are far from me.
> They ***worship*** me in vain;
>> their **teachings** are merely human rules.

Matthew 15:8-9 (NIV)

Notice the CENTRAL/PERIPHERAL, NEAR/FAR orientation: *lips* are on the border between inside and outside, far away from the center; the *heart* is at the center, and therefore the heart is more prototypical, more important, and, well, more *central*.

Notice also that *worship* is parallel to *lips* (it's the act of singing, confessing, professing, praising, not the feeling of adoration in view) while *hearts* are parallel with *teachings*. That reinforces the idea that **thinking, teaching, reasoning, and believing are all seated in the HEART.**

In our culture, when we say we believe something *in our hearts*, I think we also mean that we believe it with the core of our being. But we shade that belief toward a *feeling* or *emotion* in the heart, because the HEART is the seat of emotions for us.

In a more biblical way of talking, **"faith" is shaded toward what is CENTRAL**, which of course includes but does not preference emotions.

The Apostle Paul can say, for example:

> It is with your **heart**
> that you **believe** and are justified,
> and it is with your **mouth**
> that you profess your faith and are **saved**.

Romans 10:10 (NIV)

I gather Paul would use HEART as the seat of understanding, *and* reasoning, *and* trusting, *and* depending on Jesus (i.e. faith). Paul isn't talking about an emotional experience of the heart *as opposed to* your reason. That is, I think emotions are *part* of what comes from the heart, but HEART emotions (as opposed to GUT emotions?) are usually (always?) connected to *thinking* and *understanding* as well as emotion. **This concept of the HEART is more of a whole person, center of the person, self, soul, reason-and-emotion-together kind of idea.**

The Latin word *credo*, from which we get "creed," means "to give your heart to." I don't think the Latin Church Fathers meant "to give your *feelings* to;" I think they meant, "to give your whole thinking, reasoning, trusting, feeling, person, self, and soul to." That's what I think we mean when we say. "*Credo*; I believe in God, the Father Almighty, ..."

Back to Matthew 15, you can see pretty clearly how Jesus uses HEART to mean CENTER rather than "seat of emotions." What goes *into* the mouth originates outside a person and stays *peripheral*; just passing through; in one end and out the other. But what comes *out of* the mouth comes from the *center* of the person, and therefore reflects what the person is like, actually and truly, at their core. "For out of the **heart** come evil **thoughts** ... " Jesus says.

Again, the heart is tied to *thinking* rather than *feeling*. Or maybe better said: **the heart refers to a person's CENTER, and therefore includes thinking and understanding as well as emotion. The heart is who you are at your core, as a whole person.**

As we continue to explore the heart/soul/emotion/thinking/believing dynamic in the way the Bible talks about the whole person, my big suggestion is simply the idea that **CENTRAL/PERIPHERAL is one key element in understanding what the Bible means by HEART**. Emotions in the guts are less central than emotions in the heart. Thoughts that belong to the core of who you are live in the heart. When you have faith or even love in your heart, you have it in your CENTER, at the nexus of who you are as a person; your self; your soul.

You certainly have emotions in your heart; but maybe not *all* your emotions are in your heart. And, biblically speaking, your heart certainly contains more than just your emotions.

In our common way of speaking, if we say someone makes decisions "with their heart," we mean that their emotion clouds their reason and they "go with their gut" *instead* of their head. Our Romantic idea of "following your heart" means giving in to our feelings *against* our better judgment, our reason, and sometimes even our conscience.

But **I want to love the Lord my God with all of my HEART**; that is, from the center of who I really am, with all of my (fallen but redeemed) thinking, reasoning, imagining, trusting, desiring, judgment, conscience, and of course, emotion. And **I have the Spirit of Jesus dwelling in my HEART** (Galatians 4:6); that is, at the CENTER of who I am, and how I think, and what I trust, and how I reason, and what I believe.

When the evil things in my HEART come out and show how much I still struggle with my old, sinful self, I join King David in praying, not for a new set of *emotions*, but for a renewal of my whole person, the restoration of who I really am in Christ, the transformation of my being, my thinking and feeling and acting: "**Create in me a clean HEART, O God**; and renew a steadfast spirit within me" (Psalm 51:10)

When we read "heart" in Scripture, we should be thinking HEART: the center and most important part of a person. That's my working hypothesis, anyway. Try it out. Look for "heart" language as you read Scripture. Try thinking or praying or living out your faith as if "heart" meant CENTER and not just *emotions*. And let me know what you think. This faith thing is, after all, a grand experiment in following.

Good thing I have Jesus "down in my HEART."

33. Living with Loose Ends

By Kristeen Bruun

My son called recently to find out how and what I was doing. "I am clearing out," I told him, and I also assured him that he should be grateful to me. If I were not doing this job now, he would be stuck with it, sometime down the road, and it would likely be worse by then.

Aspects of this process are far from easy. I have to face the fact that I have left so many projects unfinished. A box of fabric, most of which still makes me go "Oooh..." as I fondle the lengths; I had plans for those.

Boxes of handwritten index cards and notebooks, representing research for papers unwritten, because my scholarly life began long before computers took over the world.

Books, of course. What was I thinking as I acquired them, each one with a purpose, occupying a niche in my thought-life? Off to the used book dealer they must go now.

Some things are relatively easy to dispose of. I'll never interview for another job, so my expensive "interview suit" can go to the local Center of Hope shop. So happy to see it go!

A set of teacher's manuals can go to the Director of Christian Education; they served me well, and may help her.

Even as I discipline myself to let go of many things, at the same time, I'm ordering a couple of books that I need. I'm teaching a four-week seminar during Advent to the Adult Sunday School class, for which I will use Martin Luther's *Christmas Book* and Justin Rossow's *You, Follow Me: A Daily Discipleship Travel Log for Advent and Christmas*. So the cycle of "letting go while collecting" seems never to end.

Although I've tried, I've never yet left a job with all of the loose ends tied up. I think this might be how we're supposed to live.

Jesus, after all, did not tie up all of his loose ends. Jesus said, "I'm sending you the Holy Spirit so you can continue on the journey and carry on the work" (John 14:16-17). Paul, writing letters to the churches he founded, certainly recognized that there was work still to be done in the communities he loved.

Like characters in a play, we enter when called, and exit when it's time. We must place our personal loose ends in the hand of God, who continues to work with us (and on us!) each day. "For I know the plans I have for you, declares the LORD" (Jeremiah 29:11).

As I continue to cull, I hope that I am letting go of things that I will no longer need, and that letting go now is part of God's plan. But I have to admit, there are books on my shelves that I have bought (and sold) more than once.

Don't worry: if I need it, God will find it for me.

In the meantime, I am living with loose ends.

34. Helpless Waiting

By Justin Rossow

This Easter I was struck by a detail I don't remember seeing before. In fact, I didn't even see it this year until my second or third reading of Mark's resurrection account. And I would have probably missed it again except for the fact that I have recently been doing some work on Sabbath and rest.

Mark 16:1 says, "When the Sabbath was past, Mary Magdalene, Mary the mother of James, and Salome bought spices, so that they might go and anoint him." Then, in verse 2, we get another indication of time: "And very early on the first day of the week, when the sun had risen, they went to the tomb."

> When the Sabbath was past, Mary Magdalene, Mary the mother of James, and Salome bought spices, so that they might go and anoint him. And very early on the first day of the week, when the sun had risen, they went to the tomb.
>
> *Mark 16:1-2 (ESV)*

I've always read that as one action: the women got up on Sunday morning, bought spices, and went to the tomb. But that's not actually what Mark says. Part of the complication is cultural: I'm not used to a day starting with sundown. I don't have "going to bed" as one of the first things on my agenda for a busy day. I start the day by waking up and getting busy. Against my experience, the Old Testament uses sundown as the beginning of a new day. That "sleep first" paradigm is a rhythm of life reminder that highlights our dependence on God for all things. But I find it more natural to think of the day starting with sunrise, so I naturally read over the reference to the Sabbath ending in verse 1 and compress it into the day starting with sunrise in verse 2.

The other complicating factor is linguistic. Or maybe it's cultural, too: culture and language are intertwined. I vaguely remember being taught (and I looked it up, just to make sure) that Mark sometimes uses Hebrew indicators for times or days, and sometimes he slips into Greco-Roman usage. It's natural for Mark and Mark's readers to live in both worlds at the same time.

So here's what's going on in Mark 16: The women have been observing the Sabbath day of rest since just before sundown on Good Friday evening when they saw where Jesus was laid in the tomb. Now, *as soon as the Sabbath was past* (Hebrew reckoning)—in other words, after sundown on Saturday night—they run out to buy spices so they can be ready to go to the tomb as soon as they can, which will have to wait until sunrise. (I'm told you can still observe a similar phenomenon in Orthodox Jewish communities today: as soon as the Sabbath is over, right after sundown on what we consider Saturday night, people make a quick grocery run to pick up items they will need in the morning but that they couldn't shop for on the Sabbath.)

So for these women, it's already Easter Sunday on the Hebrew calendar; they make a spice run to their local market but have to go to bed before they can do anything else.

Then, *very early on the first day of the week, as soon as the sun was up* (Greco-Roman reckoning), the women head to the tomb. It's a two-step process with hours of darkness in between: first, they run out to get spices as soon as the Sabbath is past; then, after the night is over, they go to the tomb.

Maybe that detail doesn't change much about the actual story of Easter. But it does highlight an important feature I would have otherwise missed. These faithful women are doing what they can, what they know to do, as soon and as quickly as they can; and still they are left helplessly waiting.

Imagine the grief and the frustration and the futility of having the embalming spices on hand, but having to wait for the light of day. Imagine how helpless they must have felt, when they could do nothing more than they had already done; when they had nothing left to do but wait.

I know that kind of frustrated, helpless, impotent waiting. I remember the phone call that said my sister had sustained a severe head injury in a car accident. The next few hours were filled with a flurry of activity to make travel plans and get on a plane and arrive at the hospital fearing I might be too late even to say good-bye. And then, after I saw my unconscious sister in her hospital bed, there came long hours of helpless waiting. Of course we prayed. But mostly we waited, because there was nothing else to do. Our complete dependence on Jesus was painfully obvious.

Recently, my friend Amy watched as her elderly father took a turn for the worse. Her family experienced a flurry of activity as details about hospice care and other medical and legal decisions had to be taken care of. And then came the waiting: days and weeks where even her dad got tired of the wait. "He's ready," she told me. "He just wants to go home."

I've watched and waited with loved ones as they have waited to die, and the sense of helplessness and frustration often reminds me of Sonnet 19 by John Milton, a famous poem by a famous poet I got to know back in my English Major days.

John Milton, already an accomplished author, went completely blind (due, in part, to his prolific writing) when he was only 43 years old. Sonnet 19 was written in response to that blindness, and is often known by its opening lines: "When I consider how my light is spent / Ere half my days …"

Milton feels helpless and useless. If he can't see, how can he write? If he can't write, what good is he? How does God expect him to do anything worthwhile if that God-given talent is buried? "Doth God exact day-labour, light denied?" Milton asks. How am I supposed to give an account of myself before God if God has allowed this blindness? Milton knows helpless waiting and complete dependence.

Milton's response to his own question has been a comfort to me. After wondering if he is off the hook for faithful service to God because of his blindness, Milton imagines God as King, and thinks of all the servants the Almighty has, and recalls that God doesn't need any of Milton's work or talent to rule the world. Then the poet sees a place in the court for those who aren't currently out on assignment for the King: "They also serve who only stand and wait."

When I am in the midst of what feels like helpless waiting, when I can't do anything but depend on Jesus, I remember Milton's words, spoken from the depth of his own helpless inactivity: "They also serve who only stand and wait."

Sometimes, the only faithful action you can take is to wait; and waiting in helpless dependence on Jesus is always a way of providing faithful service to the King.

That moment when you have nothing left to do, so you turn to Jesus and wait—that moment is a beautiful and intimate expression of faith, no matter what happens next. When we stand and wait on the bidding of the King, we don't know what form our faithful service will take. But we entrust whatever comes next to the wisdom of the King.

John Milton was right to see even his helpless waiting as a kind of faithful service. What he didn't know was how wrong he was about the end of his writing career. Milton didn't even *begin* his most famous work, *Paradise Lost*—one of the most important epic poems in all of English Literature—until *after* he was completely blind and thought he would never write again.

Not every story of helpless waiting ends the same way. Amy did eventually bury her father, and his faithful waiting for death is now a faithful waiting for the resurrection of the dead and the life of the world to come. My sister, Brooke, made a somewhat miraculous recovery from that closed-head trauma and continues to actively serve the King; her thick, curly hair completely covers the scar.

As for those women at the tomb, they give me hope in my times of helpless waiting. They did what they knew to do—they ran out to buy spices as soon as they could—and then got stuck having to wait.

In their frustration, in their grief, in their waiting, they didn't know, they didn't understand, they couldn't have imagined that their own frustrated plans would come to nothing. The spices they had rushed out to buy as soon as the Sabbath was over never got used the next morning: the dead body they were going to anoint wasn't dead anymore.

Those faithful women leave the empty tomb terrified; they don't say anything to anyone because they were gripped with fear (Mark 16:8). Their frustration and inactivity had been for nothing; their helpless waiting was misguided and misinformed; they bought funeral spices at great personal expense, but to no end. Nevertheless, the Jesus whom they loved and longed for was faithful, transforming their helpless waiting into beautiful service rendered to the King.

The resurrection of Jesus changes everything. Even if your waiting feels helpless, even if your inactivity feels frustrating or misguided, even if you are waiting for something you don't want or can't control, that helpless inaction is an expression of complete dependence on Jesus. No matter what happens next, the risen Jesus holds your future and your eternity.

When you feel helpless and tired of waiting, remember those faithful women and their superfluous spices. Remember the faithfulness of the risen Jesus. And recall the words of the poet: "They also serve who only stand and wait."

35. RAIN-ing with Jesus

By Naomi Rossow

I have been seeing my current therapist for about six months now. She is amazing, and we have been able to work through a lot together as well as explore some tools for me to use in my daily life. One of my favorites, and hers, is called the RAIN meditation. This is a self-compassion meditation created by Tara Brach, PhD.

I use the RAIN meditation most often when I am struggling with a strong emotion or need a way to look deeper into what I am feeling and why. I find it is a really helpful emotional processing tool and it has helped me practice better self-compassion. I have also had the opportunity to explore more of what the meditation means to me and how I can personalize this resource for myself.

Through this exploration, I started practicing what I like to call "RAIN-ing with Jesus." This process takes Brach's RAIN meditation and invites Jesus to be a part of it. So, let's walk through it together.

The RAIN meditation has four basic steps:

(R) Recognize;
(A) Allow;
(I) Investigate; and
(N) Nurture.

The first step is to **(R)**ecognize and name your emotions. The second is to **(A)**llow those emotions to be there without any attempt to change, fix, or judge them. The third step, **(I)**nvestigate, is meant as a place for you to explore an emotion and why it is there, what you believe about yourself because of it, and what other emotions are present. And the final step, **(N)**urture, is a place to ask that emotion what it needs to hear, and then give it that compassion. (Brach has multiple blogs and other resources related to this meditation on her webpage; you can get a more extensive understanding of each step there.)

Now that we know what each letter in RAIN stands for, we can explore how to invite Jesus into that process. When I first started thinking about this, I was thinking out loud in a brainstorming session with my dad. I mentioned this meditation and we started bouncing ideas back and forth of how to invite Jesus into it.

My original idea was to add a second (I) to the acronym to indicate "invite" into the steps of the meditation, but we quickly realized that each person has their own preferences of how to invite Jesus into a processing moment and their own individual journeys with Jesus, so we could not make a "one size fits all" way to invite Jesus into it. (Besides, "RAIIN" doesn't work as well as an acronym.)

Because of his unique walk with Jesus, my dad would rather invite Jesus into the meditation at the very beginning and have Him intentionally included for all four steps. But I would rather invite Jesus into the process during the (I)nvestigate step because of my unique walk with Jesus.

So, I encourage you to walk through this meditation with Brach on her YouTube video or blog and then explore what RAIN-ing with Jesus looks like in your unique journey.

Here is what a RAIN-ing with Jesus meditation might look like:

I like to do the meditation while sitting at my desk in a comfortable but upright position. This allows me to be focused and awake but not distracted by the TV or the temptation to lie down in bed and take a nap. It also allows me to have my computer in front of me. I like this because one way I process big emotions or experiences is journaling about it. So having my computer in front of me lets me journal as a part of the same meditation process.

After I am comfortable and able to focus, I allow myself to relax into my body. I take a few deep breaths and really notice how my body feels and let the sounds around me lull me into a focused mediation. (This is where I think my dad would like to invite Jesus into the meditation.) This process allows me to start to **Recognize** what my body is telling me and name the emotions present in the moment. The last time I did this those emotions were: anxiety, stress, and excitement.

After I name the emotions, I focus on where I can feel them in my body. I felt the anxiety in my chest, almost like a buzzing sensation. I could also feel very tiny bubbles of anxiety and excitement in my stomach. The stress made my chest and shoulders feel tight.

This noticing allows me to really get in tune with my body and emotions and helps me to **Allow** the emotions to be present. Sitting in the emotions, especially ones I perceive as bad, is the hardest step for me. My instinct for so long has been to put those emotions in the back closet of my mind and shut the door tight. I try to sit in the emotions until I feel like I am not pushing them away anymore or rushing through this step. Sometimes that can be only a minute and sometimes, mostly with more intense emotions, it can take a little while.

After I have allowed the emotion to be present and encouraged myself to sit in it, I invite Jesus into the mediation with a short prayer. That prayer for me is normally along the lines of: "Jesus, come into the experience with me. Bring Your Holy Spirit to guide my thoughts as I explore why this emotion is present and what it is telling me." Like I said before, this step can be added in wherever, whenever, and however you feel it is best and most right for you. I can't tell you when that is, only share my experience with it.

Next, I **Investigate** the emotion. I ask questions like "What else is here?", "What experience triggered this emotion or is attached to it?", "What do I believe about myself and this emotion?" This is the step I sit in the longest. I have lots of theories on why this is the step I take the most time on, but regardless of why, I find it most helpful to search underneath and beyond the surface emotion that I first named.

I kind of imagine I am walking through a tunnel, or cave, or library with lots of secret passages. I like to walk through those places in my head; as I go, I discover more things about myself and the emotion.

When I did this with anxiety a couple of days ago, I found a lot of that current anxiety stemmed from doubts about myself and my ability to succeed as a presenter at the National Youth Gathering. There was a lot of doubt about my credentials to be able to speak on the topic of emotions and faith. I mean, I am not a faith leader of any kind and I have no professional training in emotions, faith, or speaking. I also was very self-critical of the amount of work I put into the presentation because, while I have been putting a lot of work and time and thought and research into the presentation and what I wanted to say, I have also been in school and job hunting and maintaining a social life. My anxiety had latched onto these things and made me feel guilt and doubt in myself and the upcoming presentation.

This exploration leads into the fourth step: **Nurture**. After investigating my anxiety and diving deeper into that emotion with Jesus, I was able to identify some really tough things I had been subconsciously believing about myself and telling myself. To nurture this emotion and those thoughts I gave myself comfort and reassurance. I reminded myself that I was chosen out of who knows how many applicants to be a speaker. I wasn't chosen because I have all the right credentials or letters after my name. I was chosen because they liked me and my pitch, because they want to include a more diverse population of speakers, including young women. I told myself that I had lots of people backing me up and supporting me and that I was not doing this alone. The purpose of this step is to tell that emotion what it needs to hear for you to move forward, even when moving forward doesn't mean everything is okay. This can be a good place in the meditation to remember some promises from Jesus or maybe a Bible verse you hold onto.

After finishing the meditation, I like to take a few more deep breaths to center myself again and bring myself back to the present. I rejoin the world and get back to whatever work I need to do. I don't formally thank or "dismiss" Jesus like how I formally invited Him into the meditation; I like to just go back to my day, keeping Jesus and the Holy Spirit and the calm from the meditation with me.

I encourage you to try this meditation out for yourself and explore ways in which you can personalize it to your faith walk with Jesus.

36. The Day after Perfect

By Katie Helmreich

Ah, summer... Sunshine and a more laid-back routine. The kids are home doing their childhood thing. The Suburban has been packed, unpacked, and repacked for trips so often this summer that I've already lost count. Beach towels and swimsuits are nearly always laid out to dry, adding a festive touch to the front porch.

And popsicles. So. Many. Popsicles.

I love summer and all the fun we squeeze into it! I go with the flow, hang up the hammocks, pack the snack bag, and take the pictures. I'm pretty sure heaven will smell like sunscreen!

So why do I feel so stressed out and overwhelmed?

Somewhere in the sun-soaked chaos of June, my neat little stack of good habits toppled over. In embracing "laid back," I let go of a few small things. Getting up early? Hah! Journaling...? Oops. No phone scrolling before breakfast? Eesh. Yoga? Daily devotion?

So what if I miss a day (or a week) in my journal? Who cares?

But I know a few minutes journaling helps me think more clearly. And the power of writing "I'm grateful for..." and "I'm looking forward to..." several times changes the tone of my thoughts for the rest of the day.

Is daily devotion really such a big deal? Maybe not.

But the longer it's been, the harder it gets for me to identify the cause of mounting frustration, anxiety, and emptiness. So, for me at least, yeah. It matters.

It's silly, but when I have a box to check and I can see the checked boxes adding up, it's easier to stick with it. I had a little habit tracker going for a few months this spring, and it was a big help!

Did it matter that I had a 50-something-day streak going for yoga? Not really. But it sure made a difference the next morning when I was debating whether or not I had time for yoga. Same thing when it came to every other little habit I was working on!

But in June? I quit checking boxes. I didn't mean to, but I did. Since then the good habits have been dropping off, one at a time, until I've found myself floundering.

There was a time I would have beat myself up about it. I legit felt like I'd gotten important things figured out! And then I just quit doing them?!? C'mon, Katie...

Jon Acuff (a fellow pastor's kid), writes a lot about goals and habits. He writes about the fact that there will be a day after perfect. Always will be. At some point, for whatever reason, that thing you're working so hard at doing won't happen. There will be a day after perfect.

What will you do then? Quit? Or reset?

Another favorite inspiration, Dawn (from The Minimal Mom on YouTube) often chats about the fact that no system or plan will do itself. We figure out the how, and then we make it happen. But inevitably we'll fall behind; it's just part of life!

Quit? Or reset?

Paul writes a similar, encouraging message to his friends! After urging them not to be distracted by false teaching, or lured off track by the culture around them, he writes:

> But we ought always to give thanks to God for you, brothers beloved by the Lord, because God chose you as the firstfruits to be saved, through sanctification by the Spirit and belief in the truth. To this he called you through our gospel, so that you may obtain the glory of our Lord Jesus Christ. So then, brothers, stand firm and hold to the traditions that you were taught by us, either by our spoken word or by our letter.

> *2 Thessalonians 2:13-15 (ESV)*

When we get off track, whether it's in our habits or falling into harmful sin patterns, do we quit? Or reset?

We're not just trying to live good lives, stay healthy, or be successful in the things we set out to do. We are chosen and saved by God! We've been given far more than a pep talk. We've been given the Holy Spirit!

The day after perfect, the Holy Spirit will keep on sanctifying. The Spirit will continue to shape and grow our hearts and minds through daily habits, experiences, and God's Word.

The day after perfect we're blessed with the opportunity to look back and learn from our experiences. What might be behind the things that worked well in the past? Which things turned out to be only destructive distractions? Who might be blessed if I'm willing to share the fact that I screwed up, but that God was there to sanctify and strengthen me?

The day after perfect we see how much we've grown from our last set back. Those things we've learned—the ways we've changed, connections we've made, systems we've put into place—they're not gone. It may be a "two steps forward, one step back" sort of experience, but that's still growth. Even if we take one step forward and three steps back, we're far from where we began!

The day after perfect...

> May our Lord Jesus Christ himself, and God our Father, who loved us and gave us eternal comfort and good hope through grace, comfort your hearts and establish them in every good work and word.
>
> *2 Thessalonians 2:16-17 (ESV)*

Today, the day (week) after perfect, I'm grabbing a notecard and starting a new habit tracker. I'll grab a few minutes for devotion, unroll my yoga mat, pull out my journal and write: "I'm grateful for the day after perfect."

37. Created to Create, Part 1: Reflecting Beauty

By Valerie Matyas

In the beginning God created the heavens and earth.

Genesis 1:1 (ESV)

Human beings were created to create.

We are created in the image of God, the ultimate Creator, who creatively created us. We may be creative problem solvers, creative thinkers, creative designers—the list could go on—but we are all creative, in one way or another.

I have noticed, over time, that the things we humans create are often imitations or reflections of the beauty in God's creation. Take glitter for example: whether you love it or abhor it, glitter ultimately reminds us of sparkling sunlight dancing on water, or the sun's brilliant reflection bouncing off crisp, clean snow.

During an ice storm earlier this year I noticed sunlight reflecting gorgeous rainbows off the ice-encircled twigs of a tree. The effect immediately reminded me of a crystal chandelier. I couldn't help but wonder if the first chandelier (and every one created ever since) was inspired to imitate the effect of the sun on ice.

A room of romantic candlelight or a string of soft white Christmas lights reminds us of stars in a darkened sky. Perfume and scented candles point us back to God's created flora. Fireworks are imitators of the sparks released from a campfire or the explosion of a volcanic eruption.

What we humans find beautiful is often a reflection of God's artwork in creation itself; and when we create, we imitate and reflect both God's creative nature and the nature God created.

Human beings were created to create, because we were created to reflect God to the creation. Whenever you do your uniquely creative thing, you are participating in God's creative work.

You were made to reflect beauty.

In her devotion, Valerie mentioned glitter, chandeliers, candlelight, perfume, and fireworks as items of beauty that reflect God's creation. Can you think of other examples of beautiful things that are ultimately a reflection of God's creation?

Prayer

Thank you, Lord, for allowing us the opportunity to reflect Your amazing creation back to You. Thank you for creating us to be creative.

Thank you for the skills, abilities, and talents you have granted us. Continue to uphold, sustain, and nourish our love for being creative. Let it all be to Your Glory.

In Jesus' Name we pray. Amen.

38. Created to Create, Part 2: Concrete or Abstract?

By Valerie Matyas

Make a careful exploration of who you are and the work you have been given, and then sink yourself into that. Don't be impressed with yourself. Don't compare yourself with others. Each of you must take responsibility for doing the creative best you can with your own life.

Galatians 6:4-5 (MSG)

I have a beautiful painting of my grandmother's farm house hanging on a wall near my kitchen. I see it daily and am reminded of my childhood daily. I love that painting. I know the artist, I remember where it hung during my childhood, and I look forward (many years from now) to gifting it to my niece/goddaughter who currently lives in that farm house.

Every once in a while I smell a smell, hear a phrase, feel an embrace and I am reminded of my grandma. It sneaks up on me unexpectedly; it is delightful and emotional. I enjoy both the concrete and abstract reminders of her.

In the creative visual faith circles in which I walk, I have noticed two very distinctive types of artwork: one that is very concrete, and one that is rather abstract. I find both styles beautiful and edifying. Both draw me deeper into understanding or reflecting on Scripture, or allow me time to pause, focus, and have a visual reminder of what was lifted up in prayer. I enjoy dabbling in both, but find that I am not an expert in either, which allows me to hold both of them loosely.

I am very good friends with Visual Faith® artists who are extremely talented in either concrete or abstract forms of visual representation that draw the viewer in more closely for the time and purpose of understanding and meditating on Scripture. I have heard talented artists on both sides either lament, complain, or justify why they are not good at the opposite form: "I could never draw that; it just wouldn't look good," or, "Every time I try to do that it comes out a mess."

Here is what I have come to understand: The concrete artist trusts her ability to draw the subtle curve or the ocean shore. She can expertly and purposefully add color and shadow to create depth and overall beauty. She understands perspective, composition, line, and form. She can expertly execute what she sees in her mind and is pleased with the overall result of the finished product—to God be the glory.

The abstract artist trusts the process and technique required for the emotional representation she desires to convey. She may not be able to draw the ocean, but she can choose colors, patterns, and layers that convey the emotion of the ocean—tranquility, power, peace, majesty, vastness, depth, etc. She can achieve the emotion she is trying to convey and is pleased with the overall result of the finished product—to God be the glory.

Whether you excel at the abstract, revel in the concrete, or dabble in both (like me), you can allow your artwork to be a reminder of your Heavenly Father's love for you. Allow visual faith practices to draw you closer to Jesus while you are studying his Word or meeting with him in prayer. Jesus loves you, and wants to know you better; and Jesus wants you to know him.

Looking at the way other people are gifted can naturally lead to wanting to be like that, leaving the abstract artist wishing they were better at the concrete, or the concrete artist wishing they were more abstract, or the less visually expressive wishing they had more natural artistic talent. But the notion that you should be better or different than you are runs the risk of rejecting the creative way God has already made you.

Of course, you can get better. Of course, you can explore other techniques. But you never need to do something better or more to try and get divine approval for your art. You are loved; you are his; you need not waste any more time or thought comparing your work to another's.

Instead, you have an open invitation to create boldly. Your Heavenly Father will hang your artwork on heaven's refrigerator, not because of the intrinsic worth or value of your art, but because you are so valuable to him.

However concrete or abstract, however professional or amateur your art, the time you spend engaging God's Word and prayerfully spending time with Jesus through color, design, shading, wordsmithing or collaging—any way you engage God's Word is an investment in your relationship with One who loves you more than you could ever imagine.

Reflection Questions

Do you consider yourself more of a concrete artist or an abstract artist? What do you admire about each style? How can we shed the burden of the comparison game so that we can be energized and humbled in the abilities we do possess? What could be a simple phrase you tell yourself that will help remind you of the truths found in Galatians 6:4-5?

Prayer

Thank you, Lord, for my budding artistic ability.
Thank you for allowing me to grow closer to you in
Scripture and prayer through visual faith practices.

Lord, help me to remember that you have created me
fearfully and wonderfully. Give me the boldness to
creatively reflect on your truths in the way that you
have created me to.

Guard my heart from the fickle trap of comparison.
Keep my eyes and heart focused on you. Allow me to
rejoice in the gifts of others. In Jesus' name I pray,
Amen.

39. Created to Create, Part 3: Authentic Imitators

By Valerie Matyas

Therefore be imitators of God, as beloved children. And walk in love, as Christ loved us and gave himself up for us, a fragrant offering and sacrifice to God.

Ephesians 5:1-2 (ESV)

I am, by nature, a farm girl. I know where milk comes from, how eggs are produced, and I fully understand that ground beef does not, in fact, come from the ground. I can spot a real stalk of wheat from an artificial stalk found in craft stores. When it comes to anything on the farm, I can distinguish a replica from the authentic.

Recently, I had an opportunity to stay in a beautiful home on the shore of the Atlantic Ocean. I enjoyed taking multiple walks on the beach, right where the water met the sand. Littered along the coast were a variety of shells, I was amazed by the variations of size, color, texture, and shape. The house in which we lodged boasted an exuberant décor of seashells: in every corner, on every wall, upon every shelf sat countless shells ready to be admired.

The more I thought about those shells, the more I realized that I had no way of distinguishing a real shell from a factory produced shell. The shells I was most familiar with came in tidy bundles in the craft aisle of my local dollar store. Had those shells been harvested from a beach? Surely, the shells for sale had been made in a factory, right? But what was the difference??

Upon further reflection, I was ashamed to discover that my ignorance about shells led me to a ridiculous worldview that amounted to some mythical being taking factory made shells and scattering them on the shore for tourists to find. (How else do I account for those imitation shells I buy at the store just miles from my house showing up on a beach by the ocean?) I tacitly believed in some kind of demented Easter Bunny, only instead of eggs, it was seashells. Bottom line: I cannot tell an artificial shell from an authentic shell.

We are called to be imitators of Christ. We are not replicas or artificial stand-ins; we are imitators. Our job is not to be a nice decoration or to be a cheaper version of something most people can get in real life. Instead, in our imitation of Christ, we actually bear and deliver and, at times, even represent the real Jesus to other people.

We are created in the image of God and we are being transformed by the power of the Holy Spirit to be more and more like Christ so that we can be a blessing to our families, our communities, our homes, and our church. Not perfectly, of course; but authentically.

On this side of eternity, I can only imitate Christ in an imperfect way; and I can only do that because of the grace and power poured out from the Holy Spirit. When the last trumpet sounds, I will no longer have to struggle to imitate Jesus; I will naturally and authentically be Christ-like. My glorified body will match Christ's body. I will be without sin—pure, holy, blameless. I will be the genuine thing, the real deal, the very person that I was intended to be from the beginning of time.

I do not want to be an artificial Christ, a poor substitute, an easily spotted phony, there just for show with no real benefit. I want to imitate Christ, and deliver Christ, and embody Christ; not for my salvation's sake, but for the greater good of this broken creation. I may be an imperfect imitator; but Jesus, who is present in me and through me, is the real deal.

Reflection Questions

Think carefully about artificial, nature-like items found in craft stores. How do they beautifully replicate the actual item? In what ways do they fall short? How do we imitate Christ in our everyday life? In what areas might we consider being a bit more Christ-like?

Prayer

*Dear Heavenly Father, thank you for fearfully and
wonderfully making me by Your divine design.
Lord, you and I both know that I am broken. I am in
need of Your Son, my Savior. Please continue to allow
the transforming of Your Spirit, so that I can continue
to be transformed in the image of Christ.*

*In this valley of sorrow, grant me the strength and
peace to continue to be an imitator of Christ, and see
me safely to the other side. In Jesus' Name I pray, Amen.*

Small Next Steps

A life of following is only ever lived out one step at a time. It sometimes feels like the task of following Jesus is overwhelming. But the Holy Spirit is present and active not only in the big, life-changing decisions, but in the ordinary moments of your regular life.

Following Jesus isn't reserved for heroic saints who have once-in-a-generation self-control or faith the size of a mountain. Following Jesus is for regular people who mostly put one foot in front of the other, and then look up to wonder where Jesus is and where Jesus is headed. You aren't supposed to have it all figured out already.

What's your next step?

40. What Do You Need to Follow Jesus?

By Justin Rossow

What do you need to follow Jesus? That question came back to me again this week as Pastor Neuendorf and I were preparing to preach together on the Sunday before another school year begins; the Sunday of the Blessing of the Backpacks. As students pack their supplies for a new year, what might I pack that would help me be prepared for another year of faith and life? What do you need to follow Jesus?

On the one hand, the answer to that question is, quite simply, *nothing*. You don't need anything more than you already have to begin, continue, or begin again the great adventure that is following Jesus.

In fact, Jesus has already been shaping you, guiding you, serving you, and equipping you. The Spirit of Jesus has already been calling you on and shaping your next step and holding you when you fall. Everything that has happened up to the point of you reading this paragraph in a blog about following Jesus has happened under the umbrella of God's grace. You are not alone. You have never been alone. You will never be alone on this journey.

So on the one hand, you don't need anything more than you already have right now to follow Jesus, because you have Jesus, and that's all that really matters.

On the other hand, the deck seems stacked against the kind of joyful and engaging adventure I think Jesus had in mind when he said to the first disciples—when he said to you—"Follow me." When I look at my life and my culture and the lives of the people I have loved and served, **following Jesus often feels like standing on a people mover in an airport, but facing the wrong way:** you can make progress, but moving forward is way harder than it's supposed to be. And standing still is moving backwards.

Of course, according to my own sinful nature, I am blind, dead, and an enemy of God; and a corpse will only, always move in the direction of the people mover. But I have also been joined to Jesus and his death and resurrection; I am already beginning the adventure of New Creation life now, ahead of time. I am not my own, I was bought at a price, and I have the Spirit of the Almighty God dwelling in me.

Even so, taking a small next step following Jesus can still seem like an insurmountable task. Faith can still seem naïve. Faithfulness can seem silly. And standing still is moving backwards.

In some sense, that duality between faith and unfaith in my life will remain until Jesus comes again and I no longer struggle with sin in the world or sin in my own heart. At the same time, **there are concrete ways to support my faith adventure that can help me find new delight in following Jesus, motivate and equip me to take a next step, and be more aware of what the Spirit is shaping in me.**

In fact, there *must* be concrete ways to motivate and equip following Jesus, because the opposite is clearly true: we have all kinds of ways to motivate, equip, and reward *not* following Jesus in our everyday, ordinary lives.

The average church attender knows, at least theoretically, that engaging God's Word on a regular basis fuels, propels, and shapes the adventure of following Jesus. But when it comes right down to it, when was the last time you personally *had fun* reading the Bible or *enjoyed* spending time in prayer?

One reason time with God feels like a burden instead of a delight is because we often feel like we don't have any options to choose from. We train people in only one way of reading the Bible—start somewhere, read for a while, then stop—and our prayer portfolio seems limited to reciting the Lord's Prayer from memory or imitating what you see in worship when you go to church or attend online.

Without tools and options, you don't have much choice in how you read and pray, so you lack the personal delight and motivation that leads to regular, expectant Bible study and prayer.

When it comes to motivating you to *NOT* follow Jesus, your family and friends are probably a big help. Since our culture makes religion a private affair, no one in your circle of church friends talks about their struggles and joys when it comes to faith and following. They, like you, assume following Jesus must be natural and obvious, and they must be the exception, since everyone at church puts on a good face and relegates the real struggle (and adventure) of following Jesus to their private world.

The models you have for engaging people who don't know Jesus in faith conversations feel more like combat than anything else; you are trained to defend your faith or point out the flaws in their atheist logic, but you don't find either companionship or joy in that. In fact, when it comes to faith and following Jesus, you are pretty much left on your own; and being *left on your own* can feel pretty lonely.

Take stock of your external motivations and your physical surroundings and you begin to see that even your personal economy and your environment are stacked against following Jesus. You are rewarded for "productive" time by being paid for your "work" hours. Bible study, prayer, faith conversations, and service are all designated as *personal* (religion is private), *leisure time* activities (only what produces is "real work"). Then your consumer culture trains and rewards you for spending personal leisure time on entertainment (or, better yet, shopping).

The specifics of the physical world around you—your phone, your car, your desk, your computer, your TV, your kitchen, your tablet, your living room furniture, your bedroom layout—the specifics of your physical world are intentionally designed to enable (1) busy productivity and (2) constant entertainment.

It turns out, (1) busy productivity and (2) constant entertainment kill faith. Or, at least, they work actively against faith formation.

From your personal motivation and ability, to your relational support and equipping, to your external motivations and physical environment, your world is structured and organized to prevent you from finding joy and meaning in following Jesus.

So what do you need to follow Jesus? On the one hand, nothing; this journey of discovery is an adventure of grace, and the Spirit is working in you both to desire this journey and to live out your faith, one small step at a time. You don't need to bring anything more to the table than you; and you can rest in the assurance that even coming to the table in the first place was the work of the Spirit in you.

On the other hand, your faith doesn't exist in a vacuum. The momentum of most of your minutes and hours and days pulls against taking a small next step following Jesus. Standing still is moving backwards.

While struggle will always be part of the journey, we can also begin to change the momentum of personal ability and motivation. We can intentionally affect the way our relationships support and encourage faith formation. We can even take stock of the personal economy and physical environment that make some actions easy and other actions really difficult, and use them as servants of the Gospel. **We can change the direction of the people mover to make small next steps in the right direction seem not only doable, but fun.**

There is no simple, silver bullet answer for how to make a regular habit of finding joy in following Jesus. But there are some things we can actually do that help following Jesus seem more obvious and natural.

You can't replace the work of the Spirit in your life. You can notice how the momentum of your regular life is pulling you in the wrong direction, and begin to shift some of that impetus to help you more easily take a small next step.

What do you need to follow Jesus? If you're going on an adventure, you'll need **(A) a travel pack**. Just like our kids need gym shoes and crayons and other school supplies, we could make a supply list of personal skills and values—the attitudes and aptitudes—that equip you for the journey of faith.

You'll also need **(B) a "Plus One."** Following Jesus can, at times, feel like a solo quest; but discipleship is designed to be massively multiplayer. You need people in your life that help support your next step, people who will run a small experiment with you or join you on a small reconnaissance mission to get the lay of the land. We follow Jesus better when we follow him together. And God designed us that way.

Every journey needs direction and sustenance. In the same way, discipleship needs a regular connection to **(C) God's Word and prayer.** Your interaction with God's Word doesn't have to look the same as mine, and we have almost endless possibilities when it comes to engaging Scripture and prayer.

And, just like any journey, the practice of following Jesus is made up of a series of **(D) small next steps.** Put one foot in front of the other. Check for direction, but keep moving.

How do you identify (and take) a small next step following Jesus? How do you evaluate or recalibrate your journey based on your next step? How do you find the rhythm of a repeatable process that moves you forward, and how do you plan for the detours or roadblocks when you inevitably get off track? How we answer those questions will shape the kind of people we are going to be.

Jesus is not in a hurry. Jesus loves you and loves spending time with you. Jesus is absolutely delighted that you even want to consider the possibility of figuring out how to more regularly take a small next step in his direction. And Jesus is faithful; he won't leave you alone to figure this out all by yourself.

> *Come, Holy Spirit, and shape a life of faithful following*
> *in me! Amen.*

41. A New Walk

By Raelyn Pracht

I recently wanted to start a simple new habit to reach a certain step count every day. I knew two things going into this: (1) I needed to allow time in my day for at least one walk; and (2) I knew if I didn't do it at the beginning of the day, I wasn't going to do it at all. My alarm went off at 4:30AM and I was out the door to start this new program.

The neighborhood was quiet that first morning, except for a lone owl hooting atop a silhouetted tree. I noticed buzzing streetlights and warm porch lights, but I was narrowly focused on only one thing: hitting my step goal before I turned back to the house to get ready for work.

Morning two was more of the same.

When I opened my front door on the third day, however, I made a startling discovery. Jesus was actually opening a door for me, welcoming me into an amazing world I had lost sight of for a long time.

Even though my new routine had hardly even started, the experience of walking immediately changed for me. I took one step onto the porch that morning and instantly noticed the bright sliver of moon sitting directly above the house next door. Neighboring stars illuminated the clear pre-dawn sky. Suddenly, I found myself singing "God of Wonders," as if this world I was seeing was brand new.

> God of wonders beyond our galaxy
> The universe declares Your majesty
> You are holy, holy; Lord of heaven and earth

I was still thinking of the lyrics as I went on my early morning walk. The stars and moon were soon drowned out by neighborhood streetlights. Yet, I knew the night lights were still there. My exercise suddenly turned into a prayer and praise walk. Yes, I still put one foot in front of the other, but this time I didn't constantly check my pace or the number of steps I was getting. I walked and prayed, lifting praise for God's creation, inviting Jesus to walk beside me, noticing the Spirit strengthening my relationship with Jesus as I gave my first moments of the day to the Lord.

In just three days, my morning walk, which started as a mundane way to get exercise, quickly became a spiritual routine. God took something I decided to do for my own reasons and turned it into something the Spirit was using to draw me closer to Jesus.

God didn't stop there, though. God pushed me further, drawing me even deeper into an awe-inspiring world. I began taking short walks on my breaks at work. For me, those snatches of exercise were a chance to get away from the computer and get some fresh air. But for God, those brief walks were a calling, an invitation to me to use my own created self to notice the world around me. I now call these my "Take Notice" walks.

The concept is simple. As I walk, no matter the time of day or where I am walking, I purposefully take notice of the world around me. I use all five of my senses. I pay attention to the things I smell, like fresh cut grass. I catalog sounds I hear, like birds singing. I intentionally experience the taste of cold water on a hot day, the feel of a gentle breeze against my skin, and the beauty of trees and blooming flowers I see along the way.

I walk with a new intention: to take notice of the world around me and to delight in the Lord's creation. I walk to praise my Creator and to lift up my prayers. What started as a way to get a little movement in my life has turned into a beautiful and marvelous adventure that changes in each place and each time I walk. What I notice is constantly changing, but always reminiscent of the majestic beauty and awe of God's masterpiece.

These walks are a simple reminder of God's marvelous works: a start to my day, a pause in the middle of the day, and a prayer to end my day.

The next time you are on a walk, or even sitting outside, try a small experiment: purposefully use all five senses to notice the world around you. Taking time to notice God's creation around you can quickly draw you closer to the Lord through praise and prayer.

God took one small habit I wanted to start for reasons that had nothing to do with faith or following Jesus, and used that practice to invite me into a deeper and more beautiful experience than I ever expected. I wonder what other hobbies or habits God might use to get my attention or draw me just a little closer...

Keep your eyes open for God at work in your ordinary day. Jesus has a way of showing up where you least expect him just so he can spend some quality time with you. What a joy to discover God working in the most ordinary moments of your ordinary life!

God, give us eyes to see, and ears to hear,
and hearts to notice your work in our lives. Amen.

42. Check Boxes, To-Do Lists, and Following Jesus

By Katie Helmreich

Happy New Year! Did you make any resolutions? I didn't. I'm rarely one for long range planning or big goals. But I do love lists! We've had a lot of big lists in the past year, and there will be a couple hundred more in 2022. One day at a time!

The past couple years I've started keeping a Bullet Journal/Planner to get myself organized. I use the term loosely. If you google "bullet journal" you'll see a whole bunch of elaborate and beautiful examples. Mine is more a bound collection of notes and to-do lists, but it works for me, and if I have art time, I use it elsewhere.

Although I don't use my Bullet Journal for artistic expression, it's been interesting to see the impact of these to-do lists over time. I love the feeling of checking a box as each task is completed. I like being able to put the tasks down on paper, because if I try to keep them "top of mind" I find I run out of room pretty quickly. I'm an underliner and a circler, and I like to write BUY DOG FOOD in gigantic letters so I don't have to look Lucy in the eye when we run out tomorrow morning.

A good to-do list can be an empowering thing! But if I'm not careful Perfectionism will use it against me. I have to remind myself that it isn't Failure to have unchecked boxes at the end of the day.

Life at our house isn't all that predictable, and even the best days require a fair amount of adaptation. Priorities change when you pick up the kids from school and one of them bursts into tears as soon as they're safely in the car. A divide-and-conquer type evening changes dramatically when a fire call means I'm now parenting solo. Unchecked boxes are often a sign that I chose to make extra room for a heart that needed Mom or for a family that needed our firefighter.

Unchecked boxes sometimes reflect flexibility facing family needs. But sometimes unchecked boxes are evidence of some ridiculous expectations Perfectionism tricked me into.

"If you can dream it you can do it!" is all fun and games when you're in 4th grade and want to become a marine biologist. I can put "write, illustrate, and publish my first children's book" on my to-do list, but just drawing a check box doesn't make it a reasonable goal for this Tuesday. Even "Put away laundry" is an unreasonable goal some days!

I find writing things down makes it easier to spot when Perfectionism has started raising the bar out of reach. I keep a separate list for the big, long-term goals and projects and use it as a bookmark. I haven't forgotten them, but unless it's a do-able, quantifiable task, I am not putting it on my to-do list. Is it sunny and over 60? No. Well, then "paint the garage door" won't be on my list today, but maybe "write about to-do lists for the Next Step Community" will be.

Sometimes my lists reflect a belief that there are actually around 72 hours in the day. I wish doing the math were a little easier when it comes to these things, but just because "paint the basement" has fewer letters than "empty bathroom trash" does not mean it will take less time. When it comes to house projects in particular, I'm learning to take the amount of time I think it will take, and double it. (I should get "This is not Trading Spaces" on a shirt.)

Perfectionism says 24=72. That's just crazy.

Lists keep me organized. They help me identify what my options are when I'm trying to figure out what to do after Plans A-G have gone by the wayside. Sometimes lists even help me find ways I can ask for help, which (my husband will tell you) is something I need to work on.

A to-do list is a tool; it is not a measure of worth or success. I am in charge of my to-do list; my to-do list is not in charge of me. There are tasks that need to be done today as part of my role in our family, but I also know my calling often requires going off script.

It isn't efficient for me to spend half an hour or more working on a puzzle with my daughter, but right now, puzzles are an important part of my evenings. I could devote hours to learning a second language, but instead, I'm learning all about Pokémon from my son. And that's more valuable at the moment. If I read a new book every time we sat down for a bedtime story, I estimate I would have made it through 11,000 children's books so far. But if we enjoy My No, No, No Day; If I Built A Car; or Not Your Typical Dragon for 3,000 of the 11K? So be it. I'm still not tired of them, and neither is my youngest.

It's the New Year. A season of resolutions, organization, and big beginnings! Celebrate the checked boxes! Pursue the goals that God has put on your heart!

But while you tackle each new day, give yourselves a little credit for having real reasons for your unchecked boxes. A vocation can't be fully described in a to-do list. Who you are is far more than what you do. Christ is in you.

You walk with Jesus! (Even if you step on a few Legos along the way.)

The Holy Spirit will continue to guide you throughout each day and each list. I have complete confidence that you will find a happy medium between "the dishes will wait, but babies don't keep" and food poisoning (or whatever the poem is). You recognize the nudges to make room for new needs: add the things God did instead, and check them off your list with a flourish!

I know that, while I may write the to-do list, I don't actually have all that much control over the day.

We're in the hands of our Heavenly Father. The one who organizes the universe, orchestrates history, and is the author of our salvation. We'll be just fine.

I used to dread the question, "What did you do all day?" Maybe we could simply respond: "Today, I followed Jesus."

43. Enough for the Next Step

By Alli Bauck

The people walking in darkness have seen a great light; on those living in the land of deep darkness a light has dawned.

Isaiah 9:2 (NIV)

It was a normal evening in our household. The kids were down for the night, dinner was cleaned up/put away, and my husband and I retreated to our respective "wind-down" activities. By 10:30pm I had surrendered to sleep, only waking when I heard what my dream-disrupted conscience thought was my oldest son drumming on the washer and dryer. The muffled booms were actually celebratory fireworks being illegally launched around town. The blurry, black shape of my husband appeared at my bedside, gently kissed me on the cheek, and wished me a happy New Year.

And just like that, it was 2022. In a matter of seconds, all the things that were going to happen "next year" were suddenly happening "THIS year."

When it comes to the first half of January, I'm with the people who do not look forward to the changing of the calendar with enthusiasm. There's always the depressing experience of holiday hangover, when celebrations with friends and family have ended and life starts to return to normal. Then there's the bombardment of resolutions and reminders of all the ways life is not meeting my expectations (and, quite honestly, neither am I).

I ended 2021 with this prayer on my lips: "Jesus, I'm tired." That prayer wasn't followed by a request for sovereign strength or rejuvenating rest; I just wanted to confess how I was feeling physically and mentally. My new year began with a similar, simple sentiment: "Jesus, I don't know."

I. Don't. Know. I don't know where to begin or what to expect! If I'm honest, I don't know if I'm ready...

Recently, I wrapped up the second year of journeying through the Light in the Darkness hymn journal from Next Step Press. The concluding song was the title track: "Light in the Darkness" by Brooke Orozco. One of the verses from the song speaks to how I am feeling as I begin this 2022 trek:

> Strength, strength for the weary, [Christ] comes to give us peace.
> In Him we seek our refuge, apart from this world of grief.

The accompanying podcast shared a great visual. In biblical days, people used small, hand-held oil lamps to light their way in the darkness, even on treacherous paths. However, the minimal amount of illumination given off by the lamp was only enough to light one step ahead.

At first, my modern-day mentality viewed this reality as frustrating. Only being able to see one step at a time?! Really??

When I look at that situation through the eyes of faith, however, I see the blessing of focusing on what is directly in front of me, instead of being distracted by what is around me or far ahead of me. Only being able to see one step at a time becomes an exercise in trust. The Bible tells me that Jesus is the Light of the world. Jesus—the Word incarnate— is the Lamp to my feet and the Light to my path.

In this gloomy world of grief, I often struggle to navigate the unseen. My heart is anxious when I dwell on the darkness around me. But when I trust God's Word to guide my footsteps and I cling to Christ as my Light, it doesn't matter if I don't know everything.

If I'm not ready for the days to come, Jesus understands. Jesus is there, holding back the blackness, so I can see just enough to take the next step.

> Rejoice! Rejoice! For He who is God took human form
> to be our light, light in the darkness.

44. My Winter Retreat

By Rachel Hinz

January 15th, 2022. It finally snowed in St. Louis! And the magic of the winter wonderland was only magnified in that it arrived on a Saturday morning. And as a mom, the true miracle was that today was the rarest of days: a day with no sports, no school activity, no birthday party to go to ... the white of the snow outside matched the white of that little blank square on my calendar.

"My plan for today had been to finally take down our Christmas stuff in here," I told my husband as I made my morning coffee.

"Oh, but I like all the decorations up after such a hard year," he replied.

"Yeah; and now it finally looks like Christmas outside, too," I agreed. My mind began to ponder ...

Our recent Christmas break had been a lovely and quiet time back up in Michigan. While we truly treasured the chance to see family, we also experienced the sad reality that, due to COVID-related rifts on one side of the family and health issues that had progressed with a dear family member on the other side of the family, our time away had been somewhat bittersweet. We held pain and joy at the same time.

And due to how our Christmas break fell in combination with our travels, I was tired. We had a wonderful, busy time and, while we enjoyed the trip, I didn't come back refreshed. I was specifically wanting just one day to sit and rest, and have nothing planned, and do whatever I felt the urge to do.

Maybe today is my day, I thought. And this timing would be extra perfect, too. It had been a week of continued busyness and sadly, continued hurts: words that hurt within the family; even hurtful words within the Church. Add that on top of the hurtful words and attitudes on social media and out in the world ....

Why, yes! The thought of being alone in my house while the rest of the family goes out to sled sounded quite nice; quite needed.

It would be my ideal picture of comfort, too: warm and shielded from the cold outside. It's quiet. Comfortable. Cut off from the world (my phone happily put far away from me!).

Truth be told, this is my preference in winter. I am a warm-weather-lover through and through; and yet, I will happily take a day or two of snow purely for the excuse of retreating from it (that's almost an absurd admission to sit with).

I will watch from my home and admire the beauty until ...

"Mom, will you help me get my snow stuff on?" my oldest calls from the mud room.

As I zipped up his coat (since his gloves make this difficult), he asks, "Mom, you'll come out, too, right?"

His question hits my insides like a snowball. In that moment I realized I cannot stay inside forever (or at least, not for too long).

That realization comes with another mix of pangs: the pain of giving up my wants and needs because I am NEEDED outside ... Outside in the cold ... Outside in the discomfort ...

As much as I'd love to stay inside and live every day in this winter retreat, with just my dearest family and friends—as much as I wish we could cut ourselves off from the pain that lurks "out there," I know that this isolation wouldn't be good for any of us for too long. And, try as I might to keep us protected, pain and suffering would find its way inside, sooner rather than later.

My winter retreat reminds me of a time when some of Jesus' friends were with Him on a mountain. The Bible says this was six days after some hard conversations about some pretty heavy things that would be happening with Jesus. Peter, one of the friends, even got into a heated exchange of words with Jesus.

So, I bet Peter and the others were filled with some much-needed awe at just the right time on that mountain. They got to experience Jesus in a way that was so close and personal. They got to be in the warmth and comfort of their Savior.

It makes sense to me that Peter wanted to hang out in that time for as long as possible. I'm not exactly sure what he was thinking, but I understand wanting to have a shelter that contains all the goodness that God gives, and keep it there, safe and protected.

Spoiler alert: they didn't stay on that mountain. However, Jesus continued to be with them, just as He walked with them before that mountain top. And Jesus went on to do the heaviest of things: dying the worst death for the sins of everyone, everywhere. Three days later, He came out of the grave so we would never be cut off from Him.

So now, here I am: January 15th still. The house is quiet; my family is outside. I have had some time to rest.

Even more, I have some time to reflect on what Christ has done for me. This is the retreat I actually needed.

I cannot stop time on this wintry Saturday or retreat into a communal of my family and friends and cut myself off from the world. While I can see the appeal, and I surely needed a day like today, I more clearly see that Jesus is my Winter Retreat. Jesus is my Rest. Jesus calls me to Himself, and walks with me into the world outside, a world often filled with cold and hurt but never cut off from the presence of my risen Savior.

So now I will put on my twelve layers and venture into the snowy world of today and take that warmth with me. I'll share it with those I see. Then I get to come back to a warm home that still has the Christmas decorations up. My winter retreat is a good reminder that Jesus is with me, inside and out.

45. Take a S.M.A.R.T. Next Step

By Justin Rossow

Following Jesus can seem like an overwhelming challenge. Of all the things I could do, what *should* I do? Of all the steps I *might* take, which steps are actually going to help me move toward Jesus? Those questions don't have easy answers, or even necessarily a single right answer. Discovering the clear next step the Spirit is shaping in you involves a process covered in Scripture and prayer, and best done with a fellow traveler on your rope.

But **once you have an idea of a next step Jesus is inviting you to take** (getting to that point is a story for another blog), you can get better support from others and engage more fully yourself if you **express your next step in terms of a SMART goal**.

Maybe you've run into SMART goals before; my dad was teaching about them back in the 1980's. The acronym S.M.A.R.T. can stand for different things depending on the context or the training.

I have modified the concept to fit a less corporate and more discipleship setting, but the fundamental ideas remain the same. Taking a SMART next step will help you see more clearly what the Spirit is shaping in your life.

Specific

SMART next steps are *specific*. Whether the Spirit is shaping an active response or an experience of ongoing passive reception, the more concrete you can make your next step, the better. **Your own unique faith journey will put a unique twist on even the most common discipleship experiences.**

A general, "I'm going to pray for my daughter more often," is fine, but as a next step it's vague enough that you may or may not get around to it (and you may or may not even notice if you do or don't). "I'm going to pray for my daughter three times this week," is better; it anchors your activity in the realities of your ordinary life.

"I'm going to pray for my Kate next Monday, Thursday, and Friday at 8:30 am" is **even more specific, and therefore more likely to happen**. The goal is not to put a straight-jacket on your next step; rather, these concrete and specific details provide a kind of skeleton which enables movement. An amorphous blob can't take a next step (because it doesn't have feet). Structure enables movement.

As you look for the response the Spirit is shaping in you, ask if your next step is specific; concrete as well as unique.

Measurable

SMART next steps are *measurable*. You will be able to tell a week from now whether you have taken this next step, or not (yet).

Don't get the wrong idea: you're not trying to quantify your faith or turn spiritual formation into an algebraic equation; rather, you want to **articulate a next step that can either succeed or fail**. Failure is its own kind of learning, but taking an indistinct whack at a murky next step will provide little input or feedback.

Next steps can be measurable, even if they are focused on attitudes or reception. Say the Spirit is inviting you to lean into gratitude. If your next step is, "be more thankful this week," that's fine, but how will you know if you were or not? Will you be able to tell when you were most likely to respond in gratitude and when thankfulness was a struggle for you? What will you learn if you succeed or fail at being a bit more thankful this week in a general sort of way?

"I'm going to write down three things I am thankful for each day before bed and say a prayer of thanks" is more concrete and specific, and therefore more measurable. At the end of the week you will have a list of 21 reminders of your gratitude experiment. Or maybe you only actually write something down twice; then you will have some more information on the weekly rhythms of your routine that seem to regularly get in the way of thankfulness or prayer.

Gathering information like, "I find it easier to pray in the morning than at night" could be the basis for a next *next step*. "I can be vaguely thankful if I try," doesn't give you much to go on.

Make your next step an experiment in following Jesus. **Experiments need measurable data to produce insight.** So ask, "Is it easy to tell whether or not I take this next step?" If not, make your next step more measurable.

Achievable

SMART next steps are *achievable:* not doable on your own, or by your own power, or without any help from other people (or most especially, from God); yet **realistic in an appropriately aspirational way.**

Remember, this is supposed to be a *small* next step. If you wanted to train for a marathon, the first thing you would do is probably not to run a marathon. Going from zero to reading the whole Bible by Tuesday might strain a discipleship muscle or two.

Sometimes a small next step is also a big next step (like getting married or changing careers or buying a house). But those next steps will have hundreds of small steps before and after them, so they become one in a long process of following Jesus.

How do you know if the next step you aspire to is overkill? Try asking Jesus. I mean, maybe Jesus *does* want you to read the whole Bible by next Tuesday. But look at your work schedule and the hours you have to devote to Bible reading, and wonder if there is a smaller next step you can try.

Then again, **don't let fear of failure get in your way.** So what if you fail miserably at reading the whole Bible by Tuesday? Jesus is still faithful. What did you learn in the first three chapters of Genesis you actually did manage to read? What did this experiment teach you about where you are in the spiritual discipline of Scripture reading? What's the next *next step* the Spirit is shaping in you?

You might quote the Philippians 4:13 verse, "I can do all things through him who strengthens me." But Paul is talking about being content in all circumstances (see Philippians 4:11-12), not being granted supernatural reading ability to cover all 66 books of the Bible in the next 72 hours. Understanding that you don't want to put limits on God, you can still ask if you have what you need to take this next step. Is it doable in the time you have available? Is it realistic, with a little stretch? Or is it way out there and will take 50 smaller next steps to accomplish?

Don't get hung up on trying to get it "just right." But do consider whether this next step is reasonably achievable right now.

Resonant

SMART next steps are *resonant*; that is, they make your heart, mind, imagination, and will all hum the same tune.

Resonance is a physics term that describes what happens when one vibrating object (like a tuning fork) causes another object to vibrate at the same frequency (like a wine glass). Not every pitch will make every wine glass sing, but **the right frequency will cause a reverberating response.**

You're looking for a next step that feels like that. If you are living with a discipleship theme for a season (like Generosity, or Adventure, or Scripture, or Prayer), look for a small next step that resonates with that theme. If your next step feels like a burden that drags you down, keep looking. **Your next step should give you a jolt of energy and excitement.**

Of course, there's a lot of room for personal preference and individual interests. Keep experimenting with next steps and you'll find resonance comes more naturally with practice, and makes a next step seem more doable and more fun.

Maybe the Spirit is shaping a deeper experience of prayer in your life. That could feel like a chore. Who are you going to pray for and how and for how long? That helps your next step be more specific and measurable. "I'm going to pray for my wife three times before Saturday noon this week." Good work.

Now, does that next step get you energized and engaged? If not, **wonder with Jesus how you can add resonance.** "I'm going to write my wife a love note three times this week before Saturday noon and use those notes as a chance to pray." That sounds a little more interesting, intriguing, resonant.

If you are in a Season of Generosity, maybe you would buy your wife flowers this week and pray with each bouquet. If you are in a Season of Scripture, maybe you would write out a Bible verse for your wife and pray that Scripture for her. If you are in a Season of Curiosity, ask her three unique questions and use the answers as a basis of prayer.

Whatever your next step is, frame it in terms that capture your heart and imagination.

Time-Bound

SMART next steps are *time-bound.* In some ways, setting a time parameter on your next step is just another way of making it concrete, specific, and measurable. Time, however, deserves its own consideration. (Besides, who wants to take a SMAR next step?)

Remember, you are trying to take a small next step. And then another. And then another. You will see change and development over time, and sometimes not the way you expected, so **making your next step time-bound helps keep you flexible.**

If your next step is too big or too comprehensive and will take months or years to fulfill, you end up losing the benefit of a feedback loop. Next steps sometimes go sideways; that's OK. You can learn a lot about dependence and grace and needing Jesus when you completely fail at your next step.

In fact, an attitude of curiosity and adventure means **the learning is way more important than the success of any given small next step.** If your goal is to read the whole Bible in a year, it will take a whole year to see if you reached that goal or not. Break that year-long goal into smaller, more specific, more resonant next steps that help you engage the process more intentionally. Even failure brings learning, so **fail faster and learn more.**

Don't set the bar at taking your neighbors baked goods once a month for the rest of your life. Set a day in the next few weeks where you can make that happen, then talk to Jesus about how it went and what you learned. Maybe the Spirit will shape another baked goods day in your near future. Or maybe not.

If the shelf-life of your next step is vague or longer than a month, you'll lack motivation to get it done and lose the benefit of a feedback loop. Don't try to do six new things this week for Jesus; and don't only do things that take six months to plan. Get some forward momentum by putting a reasonable and specific time stamp on your next step.

***

Trying to take a SMART next step is not about being a better Christian or a super-disciple. In fact, if the concepts related to a SMART next step end up making this adventure of discovery a burden to carry or a list of rules to follow, then stop it. Go take another hundred small next steps and then come back to see if SMART next steps actually help. **The real** goal is to take small next steps more and more intentionally, and more and more often.

You see, the more we are aware of the Spirit's shaping activity in our lives, the more we consciously depend on Jesus in the course of our daily routine, the more promises from the Father connect to *the thing in front of me right now*, the more we will see what a gracious and loving and delightful God we serve.

SMART next steps are designed to help you be more intentional in your faith walk. It's OK to try and fail and get back up and try again. Just keep putting one foot in front of the other and tell Jesus about it. This adventure of following happens one small (and SMART) step at a time.

46. Courage for a Small Step

By Katie Helmreich

My 5-year-old, Jane, has been looking forward to the end of year Preschool field trip for *ages*! "We get to go do gymnastics, Mom! *Gymnastics*!!" So we carefully counted down the days. "Is it tomorrow? Tomorrow tomorrow? Or tomorrow tomorrow tomorrow?"

Today was the big day. She bounced in her car seat the whole way to the gym. She skipped from the car to the door, from the door to the mat! Then she froze.

She hadn't been expecting all the parents to be there. She hadn't been expecting the big parallel bars, the towering stacks of mats, or the unfamiliar teachers. It was too big, too scary, and too much.

It's always strange to see my self-assured, strong-willed, ready-for-anything kid shut down when in public. No logic was working, no encouragement, no kidding around. Nothing...

So I just stood there, with a 5-year-old attached to my leg. Ugh.

Gradually, she loosened her grip. Slowly, she accepted the hand of her teacher and timidly walked toward the group. Jane silently accepted her place in the row of seated preschoolers, and eventually followed a friend up the bouncy slide steps.

She tried it! And somehow scraped her leg ... so she shut down again. She hid her face; but she stayed with the other kids.

Jane meekly followed the group to the next activity, then silently refused to have anything to do with the obstacle course in front of her.

I reminded her how much she'd loved telling her siblings about the playground she'd conquered last week. I offered to take pictures so she could tell them about this! Didn't change her mind. But I could tell she was thinking about it. She watched the others take their turns, and was just about to go for it when it was time to move on.

Showing up. Listening. Baby steps. Progress.

The next challenge looked more intimidating, in my opinion, but this time she was ready. You could tell she was terrified, and she still wouldn't say a word to her teacher, but she stood up, climbed up the mat, and rode the zip line across the room!

The next turn was easier. The turn after that she was even starting to smile and scrambled up the ramp to get back in line with gusto!

The rest of the morning was still challenging. But Jane found her courage in baby steps, trying new things, following her teacher.

To be honest, it took me a bit to get over my exasperation at the clingy-kid stage. I had to laugh my way through the idea that I'd given up my morning to stand here in a gym watching my kid refuse to do anything. But as I watched her grow into a new situation I started to realize how many things in life are like this.

I know I've often faced tasks or roles that have seemed too big, too scary, or too much! Some of the things that made me freeze probably seemed laughably easy to someone else. What's the big deal?

The obstacles we face and the ways we approach them are unique. When we follow Jesus, there will be times when we feel like skipping from the car to the door, from the door to the mat!

Sometimes we freeze. Who better to cling to than Jesus?

After a bit we're able to take a tiny step forward, often when someone comes alongside us and walks with us for a while. Following Jesus together is such a blessing!

Sometimes following Jesus just means staying, even when it's scary. When we sit on the mat, in the pew, or at the table, we learn by observing and slowly find courage by seeing how God is working in the lives of our friends.

Following Jesus doesn't always mean we're moving forward quickly. But our Savior knows just how to encourage us, and how to direct our hands and feet to the next rock on the climbing wall. He calls us by name and calms our terror just enough for us to take the next step.

Soon, as we gain momentum, and rack up a few moments of bravery, we find ourselves smiling again. We find the strength to run toward the next milestone! We flash a thumbs up to those cheering us on. We get that rush of joy that only comes on the other side of what seemed impossible!

Jane had "the best morning ever!" She was so proud! And I'm proud of her, too; especially because I know what she had to overcome!

I'm proud of you for following Jesus today! For clinging to Jesus, for showing up, for staying engaged when things get tough. And I'm so glad to be able to cheer for you along with your other brothers and sisters in Christ.

You're doing it! Sure you're terrified sometimes! It's not easy following Jesus. But by the grace of God, by the power of the Holy Spirit, here you are: doing it!

Rejoice in the moments of bravery you've experienced. Grab the hand of someone near you, and take the next step together as you continue to follow Jesus!

47. Mary and Martha, GPA or GPS?

By Justin Rossow

A couple of weeks ago, I got to lead a Next Step workshop at a congregation outside Buffalo, New York. As part of the visit, I was invited to preach in Sunday worship. The Gospel for that day was the story of Mary and Martha from Luke 10. I wanted to connect my Sunday preaching with the Saturday workshop and, although I didn't have to stick with the reading assigned for the day, Luke 10 seemed like a great way to lean into the difference between thinking about following Jesus in terms of a GPS instead of (our more typical approach) a GPA.

In the story, Martha isn't just too busy or too hectic: she is busy *doing good*. She is serving Jesus. She is being a good hostess. She is living out her faith. But living out her faith has become a burden.

I guess I've seen that burden of being a good Christian often enough to know that part of my own personal calling, in preaching or writing or talking to other people, is to relieve the burden of being a Christian with the joy of being a follower.

So I spoke on both Saturday and Sunday about shifting from a GPA attitude that checks how well I am doing and compares myself with others, to a GPS attitude that asks, "Where am I right now? And where is Jesus?"

One of my favorite moments of the weekend was the children's message. The congregation was in the middle of a sermon series on being anchored and not drifting away from your faith (see Hebrews 2:1), so I hid an anchor behind the pulpit and brought it out as the children took their seats on the front steps.

I asked one of the smallest and most determined little girls there to help me, and she gladly stood next to me and took the anchor when I handed it to her. It was a bit of a struggle for her to keep it off the ground, but she managed. Just.

I went on to explain what anchors are and how they worked, getting ideas from the kids. Every now and then I would encourage the little girl to hold the anchor up higher so people could see. The first time I asked, you could hear some chuckles in the back. I ignored the chuckles and just kept talking about anchors. I asked her again to hold it just a little higher. She struggled to comply; I ignored her and just kept talking. More chuckles and a few LOLs.

I pushed it about as far as I dared, and then relieved the little girl. Then we talked about how heavy the anchor was and how an anchor is not designed as a weight for you to carry around. Instead, an anchor is supposed to hold you in place if you start to drift away.

So I put down the anchor and asked my little helper to hold onto the rope. Then I took her hand and asked the kids about crossing the street with a parent or teacher. I asked if their mom would ever let go in the traffic, and they all said no.

So I held my little helper's hand as she held the rope and told her the most important thing I wanted the people to hear all weekend: **trusting Jesus isn't a burden to carry, it's a promise to hold onto; and Jesus will never let you go.**

That's the difference between Mary and Martha in Luke 10 (Martha shows a different side in John 11): Martha is carrying around the anchor while she vacuums; Mary is holding onto (and being held) by Jesus.

Off the Beaten Path

The scenic route is seldom the fastest or most efficient way to travel; but you get the best views if you are willing to take the occasional detour off the beaten path.

From old beer commercial lingos to angelic staff meetings, from techno-idolatry to miracles that sound like click bait, this section includes some unusual perspectives. But sometimes you can see the truth best when you are looking at it slant.

48. Ashes and Curtains

By Justin Rossow

"Dust you are and to dust you will return." Those words, spoken to Adam in Genesis 3:19, come right after the Fall. They are words of judgment; words of banishment; words of mortality. We speak them as part of the Internment Service at the graveside.

The coffin is lowered into the grave or placed in its resting place.
Earth may be cast on the coffin as the pastors says:

We now commit *his/her* **body to** *the ground/the deep/its*
resting place; **earth to earth, ashes to ashes, dust to dust …**

"Dust you are and to dust you will return." On the heels of those words, Adam and Eve are banished from the Garden of Eden. Having eaten from the one forbidden tree, they are now removed from the Tree of Life, lest they should live forever in their sin.

And the LORD God said, "The man has now become like one
of us, knowing good and evil. He must not be allowed to
reach out his hand and take also from the tree of life and eat,
and live forever."

So the LORD God banished him from the Garden of Eden to
work the ground from which he had been taken. After he
drove the man out, he placed on the east side of the Garden
of Eden cherubim and a flaming sword flashing back and
forth to guard the way to the tree of life.

Genesis 3:22-24 (NIV)

Much later, the rebellious descendants of rebellious parents find themselves wandering in the wilderness. God chooses to go with these sinful people; yet even then, the separation is evident.

God's very presence dwells in, with, and under the glory cloud that fills the Tabernacle. The Holy of Holies (or Most Holy Place) becomes the location where heaven meets earth, where God promises to be. But a curtain 60 feet tall and 4 inches thick divides the presence of a holy God from these sinful human beings.

Just as cherubim guarded the way back into Eden, the curtain depicts an angelic, heavenly host; a Keep Out sign for all who still have the stain of sin, the reek of rebellion. Banishment from God's presence is woven into the very fabric of the Tabernacle, and later, the Temple. God comes to be present, and we still are on the outside, looking in.

When the Word became flesh and *tabernacled* among us (John 1:14), the Almighty God came veiled in human form. Jesus is the place where heaven meets earth; where the eternal meets the mortal; where God again dwells among us.

In a sense, Jesus pulled back the curtain; God was again present with people, face to face. Creation was restored. Sickness, healed. Even death was undone.

One of my favorite, and most neglected, resurrection stories in the New Testament comes in Matthew 27:51-53. When the crucified Jesus cries out in a loud voice and gives up his spirit, Matthew records:

> The earth shook, the rocks split and the tombs broke open.
> The bodies of many holy people who had died were raised to
> life. They came out of the tombs after Jesus' resurrection and
> went into the holy city and appeared to many people.
>
> *Matthew 27:51b-53 (NIV)*

It's like the grave has started to leak. Death can't hold all the captives in. The original curse from the original Garden has begun to come unraveled. The separation is tearing at the seams. Indeed, with the death of Jesus, God the Father tears up the Keep Out sign that blocked the way to relationship with God.

> At that moment the curtain of the temple was torn in two from
> top to bottom.
>
> *Matthew 27:51a (NIV)*

That violent tearing counts as an act of judgment on us human beings who always misuse the ways God chooses to come to us. The ripping apart of the cosmic scene on that curtain combined with the earthquake that shook the unshakeable bedrock of the mountain takes us back to Isaiah 6, where the prophet sees the angelic host, not embroidered in gold, but soaring back and forth and shouting to make the Temple shake: "Holy, Holy, Holy is the LORD of heavenly armies!"

Like Isaiah, we respond to God's judgment on everything we think is solid and stable in our lives with a *"Woe is me! I am undone! For I am a person of unclean lips and I live among a people of unclean lips!"* (Isaiah 6:5).

But lean in a little farther. The tearing of the Temple curtain is an act of judgment; but it is also more. The same Isaiah who felt the Temple mountain shake will later promise:

> [The LORD] will swallow up on this mountain
>   the covering that is cast over all peoples,
>   the veil that is spread over all nations.
> He will swallow up death forever;
> and the Lord GOD will wipe away tears from all faces,
>   and the reproach of his people he will take away from all
> the earth, for the LORD has spoken.

Isaiah 25:7-8 (ESV)

The tearing of the Temple curtain is also the first rip in the shroud of death that veils all humanity. With that first gash, the grave starts to leak. Three short days later, the earth will shake again (Matthew 28:2), and another grave—a garden tomb, locked with an impossibly large stone, guarded by soldiers, and sealed tight—will tear open, and Jesus will step into resurrection life, the firstfruits of the New Creation.

Jesus has granted us access to the Father; through the rending of his body, we can already now enter into the very presence of the Almighty God.

> Therefore, brothers and sisters, since we have confidence to
> enter the Most Holy Place by the blood of Jesus, by a new
> and living way opened for us through the curtain, that is, his
> body … let us draw near to God with a sincere heart and with
> the full assurance that faith brings.

Hebrews 10:19-20, 22 (NIV)

This Ash Wednesday, you may join in the ancient practice of receiving ashes on your forehead in the sign of a cross. If you do, you may well hear the words of the curse, the words we still use at the internment of bodies that belong to people we love: "Dust you are, and to dust you shall return."

But the sign of the cross also points you forward. That cross marked the Beginning of the End, just as the resurrection of Jesus marks the Beginning of the New Beginning. Death has been torn asunder. The way to the presence of the Father is restored. Jesus already tabernacles with you. And yet, we still stand at the gravesides of people we love.

Let me tell you a secret: as long as a single body of someone Jesus loves is still in the grave, his work isn't yet complete. Jesus loves your body. Jesus died for your body. Your body is going to rise.

That's why, right after we say, "ashes to ashes, dust to dust," the Internment liturgy continues:

> May God the Father, who created this body;
> may God the Son, who by his blood redeemed this body;
> may God the Holy Spirit, who by Holy Baptism sanctified this
> body to be his temple, keep these remains to the day of the
> resurrection of all flesh.

The cross of Jesus means that God tore up the Keep Out sign. The resurrection of Jesus means you will walk out of your tomb, too; and in the New Garden, the New Paradise, the New Creation, you will dwell in the very presence of God.

There will be no more need for Temple curtains, veiling the presence of a holy God from sinful people. In fact, you won't need any kind of temple, sanctuary, or church building, for you will live inside a New-Creation-sized Holy of Holies, where with resurrection eyes you will see God face to face.

As you receive your ashes, remember you are dust; as you wash off your ashes, remember you are destined for resurrection.

49. Money, in a Fish

By Kim Longden

When my oldest son was little, we read from *The Beginner's Bible* each night at bedtime. One night we opened up to a story entitled "Money in a Fish" based on Matthew 17:24-27. On the last page of this obscure account was a picture of the smiling disciple Peter holding a fish with a coin in its mouth—just enough money to pay the temple tax.

I remember shaking my head and thinking *The Beginner's Bible* had jumped the shark, making up this weird story that I had never heard before. So, I looked up the reference in the Bible, and to my surprise, there it was!

Recently, the "Money in a Fish" section of Matthew came up in family devotions. I dug out T*he Beginner's Bible* and told the kids about the first time I read this story to little Micah wondering whether it was actually in the Bible.

I mused inwardly over this ongoing phenomenon—how oftentimes I am learning right along with the kids while teaching them. Then I realized there was a lively theoretical discussion going on around me: *How did the money get into the fish?*

I had never put that much thought into HOW the money got in the fish; I just thought it was bizarre that it was there. I listened to the kids' creative speculations: "A sightseer was out walking by the lake one evening," one of the kids was saying, interrupted by another, "...he was tossing coins into the lake making wishes..." Another chimed in, "The fish thought the coins were bread so it gobbled them up, like those fish in ponds that will eat anything!"

I liked this scenario as it unfolded. It all seemed so casual and commonplace; except that Peter would then catch *this very fish* with *just what he needed*, showing that it didn't all just happen randomly.

The money in a fish prompted a discussion on the ways God has provided for our family needs, big and small. In some recollections, we could trace along the threads of what we knew far enough back to see that God had set the wheels in motion to provide for us long before we even had the need.

As we reminisced, I remembered how I had worried over these situations, wondering how everything would work out. It was remarkable to see that, although there were so many unknowns during those times, nothing was unknown to God. In fact, God had been working on our behalf long before I knew there would be anything to worry about!

> No eye has seen any God besides you, who acts on behalf of those who wait for him.
>
> *Isaiah 64:4 (ESV)*

It is so reassuring to know that the same Jesus who is the commander of the winds and waves also rules over random chance for the benefit of His redeemed! It is truly amazing when the Spirit gives us a small glimpse of the beautiful tapestry God is weaving with what feel like haphazard threads in the situations of our lives and the lives of others.

God uses many hands, many means, and many channels to provide for us. Ultimately, whatever we receive by divine command or arrangement is all received from our Father's hand—like Peter's just-enough-money in a fish. Every good and perfect gift is from above! Jesus uses both the magnificent and the ordinary to grow our faith and trust in Him.

Maybe Jesus made money miraculously appear in the fish's mouth; or maybe God worked through a haphazard chain of seemingly unrelated events, eventually leading to the fulfillment of Peter's need. Either way, that coin in the fish's mouth reminds me that we can trust Jesus in everything, even in seemingly random events in our seemingly random experience. Our Creative Provider is working on our behalf!

50. A Pressed Penny Promise

By Justin Rossow

I was really struck by the Old Testament lesson this week, and glad when the preacher chose to use those strange and wonderful verses as the basis for his sermon. At the heart of that reading stands a proclamation of judgment tempered by a promise of restoration.

> And the Lord said:
> "Because this people draw near with their mouth
>   and honor me with their lips,
>   while their hearts are far from me,
> and their fear of me is a commandment taught by men,
> **therefore, behold, I will again**
>   **do wonderful things with this people,**
>   **with wonder upon wonder;**
> and the wisdom of their wise men shall perish,
>   and the discernment of their discerning men shall be hidden."
>
> *Isaiah 29:13-14 (ESV)*

The promise of restoration, of the deaf hearing and the blind receiving sight, comes a few verses later. Usually, I would think of those kinds of miracles as "wonders." But the "wonders" in verse 14 are amazing works of judgment.

This unfamiliar and unusual use of the word led the preacher to explore how we use "wonder" in our typical ways of talking. The Seven Wonders of the World cause "wonder;" that is, an emotion of awe at the magnitude or greatness of something. We can also "wonder" about something we don't understand. And if something is "wonderful," for us it is good news.

But the "wonderful" things in this text are like the 10 Wonders (that is, the 10 *Plagues*) God visited on Egypt: they certainly cause amazement, but they are definitely not good news.

Since the sermon mentioned "awe" as one of the positive emotions related to wonder, I was thinking about "awe-inspiring" verses "awful." Something that makes you "full of awe" can be an amazingly good thing; but "full of awe" can also be "awful," something amazingly bad. Wonder works a bit like that.

Connecting our experience with "wonders," the preacher talked about all the wonderful places his family visited this summer, all the sights and tourist traps and "world's greatest" designed to inspire awe (as well as souvenirs).

Later in the sermon, he mentioned a "pressed penny." You know pressed pennies, right? You put your penny (and your dollar...) into a machine and turn the crank; the machine stretches and presses and engraves an image on the soft copper of the penny. The result is a souvenir reminder of where you have been and what you have seen. They have pressed penny machines at national parks, tourist attractions, and other attractions. I last saw one at the Henry Ford Museum.

That image of a bright penny pressed and marked as a keepsake and reminder really caught my imagination. I know the cold weight of a pressed penny in my hand. I know the excitement of carrying a pressed penny in my pocket. I have seen the allure of the pressed penny machine and watched my son get caught up in the wonderful workings of that marvelous machine.

I was still thinking about pressed pennies when the sermon took us to the cross, that wonderful place of awful judgment and awe-inspiring love. I couldn't help but imagine the suffering of Jesus as he was pushed down, stretched, marked, and crushed for our iniquities. I thought of the scars the Risen Lord bears as souvenirs of his love, evidence that my Jesus has "been there, done that" when it comes to suffering, even death.

The preacher talked about the experience of suffering in my life and about the awful things that make me wonder how God could be loving; that make me think maybe the Divine Potter doesn't know (or care) as much as I thought. I imagined my own suffering like the workings of a penny press, and I thought of the Apostle Paul's words:

> We are hard pressed on every side, but not crushed;
> perplexed, but not in despair; persecuted, but not abandoned;
> struck down, but not destroyed.

2 Corinthians 4:8-9 (NIV)

Our suffering marks us; it shapes us; but we are not left alone in that shaping. Even suffering is held under the protective shelter of grace. Paul continues,

> We always carry around in our body the death of Jesus, so
> that the life of Jesus may also be revealed in our body.

2 Corinthians 4:10 (NIV)

You who have been baptized have been joined to Jesus' death and resurrection. As one who bears the sign of the cross on your forehead and on your heart to mark you as one redeemed by Christ the Crucified, you also carry in your body scars that belong to this present, fallen creation. You know the ravages of sin and aging on your body, as you experience death ahead of time. But you do not bear those signs of suffering alone.

You suffer with Jesus. You carry around the death of Jesus in your body for a purpose: that the life of Jesus may also be revealed in your body. You experience New Creation life, ahead of time.

After the sermon, we celebrated communion, and I couldn't help but notice the sign of the cross baked into the communion wafer. As I helped distribute the host, I felt as if I were handing out pressed pennies, signs and souvenirs that say "I've been there, seen the wonder, and remember the awe."

But communion isn't just about where we have been; it's about where we are headed. We can talk about the Lord's Supper as a "foretaste of the feast to come." In a very real sense, we participate in a future reality as we break the bread and drink the wine now, ahead of time. That small wafer of bread marked with the sign of the cross is a pressed penny promise; a souvenir from your future; a sign, token, and participation in the life of the world to come.

Of course, Jesus didn't have any pressed pennies. But the official coinage of the day carried the image and inscription of the Roman Emperor. You remember how they tried to trick Jesus into saying something that could get him arrested: "Is it lawful to pay taxes to Caesar, or not?" In response, Jesus asks to see a common coin. "Whose image and whose inscription does this pressed penny bear?" Ironically, the inscription pressed on the coin Jesus is talking about would likely have claimed Tiberius Caesar as both high priest and Son of God.

"Since this common coin bears the image of Caesar, give it back to Caesar," the true Son of God says. "But give to God that which is God's–that which is imprinted with God's image." That means you.

As a human being, you have been created in the image of God. That image has been marred and defaced by sin, but you still belong to the One whose image you bear.

Joined to the death and resurrection of Jesus, you belong to God all over again. You belong not only to the fallen creation, but to the New Creation. You carry in your body the marks of the death of Jesus, so that your body might also carry around the sign of the resurrection of Jesus. You are a pressed penny that shows where you are going and to whom you belong.

That's what I'm taking from worship into my week. As I notice and wonder about suffering in the world and in my own life and in the lives of people I love, I will remember that pressed penny, and remember the cross, and remember the promise of the New Creation. I will think of my own scars differently, and hold them at the foot of the cross. I will ponder the scars on the hands and feet of the Lamb who was slain, but now lives forever and ever.

In moments of my life this week that are awe-inspiring or down-right awful, I will dare to pray the words of the hymn:

> On my heart imprint Your image,
> Blessed Jesus, King of grace,
> That life's riches, cares, and pleasures
> Never may Your work erase;
> Let the clear inscription be:
> Jesus, crucified for me,
> Is my Life, my hope's foundation,
> And my glory and salvation!
>
> *Lutheran Service Book, 422*

51. A Field Guide to Humans

By the Archangel Michael, transcribed by Conrad Gempf

My fellow angels! How resplendent you all look! Can I just say, I am so grateful to you all for this spectacular turn out … give yourselves a little round of applause. We'll be going out Christmas caroling soon, and I think those shepherds will really get a little glimpse of what the heavenly host is like and how we can sing. Thank you so much for being here.

Before we head into that tiny puddle that the humans call "The Universe," I thought it would be good just to remind you of a few of the basics. I want to talk to you about the *glory* of human beings, but first, we need to touch on practical matters relating to their *limitations*.

First, I know some of you have visited before, but even the most experienced of us can be taken aback at the alien appearance of the human beings. You need to remind yourselves: they cannot harm you. Remember how limited and inexperienced they are in their present form. They will believe you can hurt them!

So try to fix this in your minds: they are going to be much more afraid of you than you are of them. In one of my visits, I neglected to adjust my appearance and … the poor human! He was beside himself with fear! All he could babble and write about for weeks were wings and eyes and "wheels." No matter how anxious you are feeling, it's wise to make it a rule to always start by saying to them (and to yourself), "Do not be afraid."

Second, it's right for us to be sensitive about language when we're in their space/time continuum. These are *gendered* creatures, who marry and are given in marriage, so remember to use appropriate pronouns. Joseph and Zechariah are he/his; Elizabeth and Mary are she/hers; and shepherds and the sheep are they/theirs. Even if they all look alike to us, the Lord sees them as individuals and we should take their individual identity seriously.

Third, remember that these creatures are, for this part of their lives, trapped in only a single dimension of time and only three of the spatial dimensions.

Think of it—only one dimension of time … and they feel like they're being constantly pushed along it … and in the same direction! In space, they know of breadth and depth as well as length, but of time, all they know is *length.*

So out of all the many features of time and eternity that are natural to us, really the only one that they understand is Sequence—one thing after another. And, only experiencing their reality this way, they honestly believe that cause and effect must be slavishly glued to sequence. So when we or their prophets try to tell them about Jesus's birth, they think we're, like, *predicting* something that hasn't happened yet, rather than talking about the centerpiece of all causes in their creation and beyond.

You'll find this hard to believe, but their understanding of the other facets of time are as much a mystery to them as their sense of taste is to us! When you talk to a human being about eternity, you might as well be talking about the scent of lemons to a regular being like us!

And their spatial perception isn't much better. Just try to think what it would be like if you could only look up & down but not look *kata* or *ana*—or if you could only look left & right but not *bithersnap* & *pinglid.*

When sometimes it seems like they cannot see the truth *pinglid* the nose on their face, remember that *they literally cannot.* Often the things we're talking and singing about will be brand new to them, things that they cannot perceive and will not have seen coming.

But this leads me to the ways that humans are so astoundingly glorious to us. Are you confident that you would love, believe, and trust like that if you'd never seen the shining glory of God's presence? — if you couldn't simply turn 16 of your eyes and behold the LORD?

Humans have to more or less *blindly* trust and believe. Literally every direction that they can turn, all they see with their eyes is dirt, sheep, neutrinos, and Higgs-Boson particles. —Oh, no, come to think of it, at this point in their existence they can't even see dark matter or dark energy! —But my point is: the poor things are practically blind! And yet they are able to love the Creator that they cannot physically see, and love in ways we can barely imagine.

Mary, for example—bless her! You see her when Gabriel first spoke to her—notice how he remembered to say, "Do not be afraid"? He was in the presence of the *Theotokos* herself, and yet he remembered that she, too, would be scared. Good work, Gabe.

You see how ephemeral and fragile she is? This is because at this point, Mary is young (even for a human). Can you believe it? Mary is *less than a thousand years old* at this point. Given her human limitations, she has no memory of anything before she was "born," only what other humans tell her.

And, of course, things ahead of her in her one dimension of time are invisible to her as well … they might as well not exist for all she knows!

So you see how she reacts to Gabriel's announcement—all of which is new to her. His news is in five stages: (1) you are going to have a child; (2) his name will be Jesus; (3) he will be called son of the Most High; (4) he will get the throne of David; and then (5) he will reign forever with a kingdom that will never end.

Now, when you think about their limitations, you'd imagine that a human like Mary would be most surprised at number five, reigning forever. But no. Five stages, and Mary is stuck on number one. (1) There'll be a baby; (2) his name Jesus; (3) his connection to Most High; (4) his kingship and (5) his eternal reign—and Mary replies to Gabriel, "Wait … I'm going to have a baby??"

But then she adjusts—can you comprehend this? I can't. Everything a human knows is limited in time and space, so it is understandable that their first thought about anything new is how it fits with them, in their time and space. But humans have these astonishing superpowers of faith and love that enable them to quickly move past limitations which would paralyze us! By the end of that very same conversation, Mary is saying, "I am the Lord's servant. May your word to me be fulfilled."

And then within days—days!—she visited her fellow human Elizabeth, and somehow Mary has understood. HOW??!?!?! "My soul glorifies the Lord and my spirit rejoices in God my Savior!" Totally unable to see it with her own eyes, yet she trusts and says, "He has been mindful of the humble state of his servant but from now on all generations will call me blessed."

HOW does Mary know about *that*? Gabriel didn't tell her, and she can't see it directly. How can a being with such limitations express such insight, such love, such trust? Amazing. These mortals are beyond the comprehension of any merely eternal being like us.

And then Mary is somehow wise enough to link the things going on in her narrow slice of time to the things our Lord has always done, is always doing. Wow.

I know that like me, all of you angels have been memorizing these amazing words from her song: *"His mercy extends to those who fear him, from generation to generation. He has performed mighty deeds with his arm; he has scattered those who are proud in their inmost thoughts. He has brought down rulers from their thrones but has lifted up the humble. He has filled the hungry with good things but has sent the rich away empty."*

How wonderful to be able to perceive and love the Almighty like this! She has never seen God, yet she paints a clearer picture than you or I.

Remember, Mary is so fragile; and yet she knows the Lord this well. She is handicapped, unable to navigate most of time and space, and yet she knows the Lord's timeless truths and somehow apprehends God's timeless character, and loves the Most High with a devotion so pure and total. And she is not the only one.

How do humans do this? You and I, mere angels, will never know. It's as if they're somehow able to fix their limited eyes on things unseen to them. But I'll tell you this much: we have as much to learn from them as they have to learn from us.

May we all begin to demonstrate that kind of faith, trust, and love, in all of our dealings. But right now, we've got some shepherds to wow! Let's go!

52. The God in My Pocket

By Justin Rossow

A friend of mine has a collection of artifacts from the Holy Land in his office, including a woven basket full of household gods. These crude figurines are replicas of actual pieces found in digs around the Middle East. Each god is unique and all appear to be imminently portable; these are gods that can fit in your pocket.

A portable deity makes good sense for a nomadic people. We know these handy idols were used for divination; that is, you could consult your pocket idol when you were out and about and really needed to know what your god was thinking (Zechariah 10:2 and Ezekiel 21:21, for example, both tie household gods with this kind of seeking divine input in order to make decisions about the future).

When God called Abram to leave his family and go to a land of promise (Genesis 12), that commissioning was also a call to leave not only his father Terah behind, but Terah's gods as well (which is exactly how Joshua would later recount the story of Abraham in Joshua 24).

But old god habits die hard. When Abraham's grandson, Jacob, finally got to marry Rachel and head back home, Rachel took her father Laban's household gods with her for the journey (Genesis 31). We can't be sure what exactly Rachel was thinking, but Laban was also a descendent of Terah, and you can imagine a direct line to your family deity might be a useful thing to have in your pocket if you were heading out on a long journey into the unknown.

The One True God renews the promise first made to Abraham and Isaac to Rachel's husband, Jacob, and in Genesis 35, Jacob gathers the foreign gods from all the saddlebags and back pockets of his entire caravan and buries them all. And that should have been the end of it. But, of course, it wasn't.

Generations later, when Jacob's twelve sons had become the Twelve Tribes of Israel; after centuries of slavery; after the miraculous Exodus that pitted the Great I AM against all the gods of Egypt (who are not); after Sinai; after "Thou shalt have no other gods in my presence;" after the Golden Calf Incident; after 40 years of eating manna in the wilderness; after Moses was buried in sight of the Promised Land and Joshua took up the mantle of leadership; even then, as God's people were about to re-enter the land promised to Abraham so long ago, Joshua has a *come to Jesus* moment with God's people:

> "Now fear the LORD and serve him with all faithfulness.
> Throw away the gods your ancestors worshiped beyond the
> Euphrates River and in Egypt, and serve the LORD. But if
> serving the LORD seems undesirable to you, then choose for
> yourselves this day whom you will serve, whether the gods
> your ancestors served beyond the Euphrates, or the gods of
> the Amorites, in whose land you are living. But as for me and
> my household, we will serve the LORD."
>
> *Joshua 24:14-15 (NIV)*

And, as you might expect, even that rededication wasn't the end of household gods or idolatry in the history of God's people.

The whole idea of a clay replica that gives you insight and hope for the future, and helps you make important decisions, and gives you direction in life—that all seems so distant and removed from my regular, everyday experience.

Until I realize that I keep something in my pocket that gives me insight, that helps me make important decisions, and often makes me feel like I have direction in life (often, literally!). When it dings or buzzes, I feel connected, like I have a purpose. Sometimes, in the dark, at night, I will stroke that little household god, scrolling through the latest news or Facebook posts.

"What are we looking for when we browse on our phones late at night?" another friend asked me several months ago. That question stuck with me, and comes back to me when that white glow of my phone creates an unholy halo around my head late at night. What are we looking for, if not for purpose, direction, meaning—something only God can really give?

My own actions seem as ridiculous to me today as those ancient nomads with clay idols in their pockets. Why *wouldn't* I be looking for meaning, or healing, or hope, or purpose in Scripture and in prayer? Why do I hold onto the weak promise of iDivination or iHope for the Future?

That's just the way of household gods, I guess. We carry them around in our pockets, assigning them purpose and power and a measure of control over our lives, without even realizing what we are doing.

"I want to read the Bible more regularly," my friend told me today. "But this thing,"—and here he pulls his own household god out of his pocket—"this thing is always near me, and telling me what's important, and what I need to pay attention to *right now*. And it gets in the way!"

Knowing that my phone can get in the way of my relationship with Jesus doesn't suddenly make it easy to set my phone down or leave it in the other room. I'm reminded of the scene in J. R .R. Tolkien's *The Fellowship of the Ring*, when the old Hobbit Bilbo is finally cowed into leaving his golden ring behind (as Bilbo himself had been intending to do). Yet, even after he decides to put it down and leave it, the precious ring mysteriously finds its way back into Bilbo's pocket. My phone is altogether too much like that.

Of course, cell phones aren't inherently evil. And of course, anything that gives you direction and purpose and hope that isn't the God and Father of our Lord, Jesus Christ is a kind of idol. So maybe that famous Bible verse from Joshua 24 is something more than a one-time commitment or a slogan for a T-shirt.

I'm not going to ask you to bury your phone under the terebinth tree near Shechem (like Jacob did with the portable pocket gods of his whole household). But I do invite you to consider again today how much of your identity is wrapped up in your portable device.

Then keep dedicating yourself to finding your true identity in your relationship with the One True God. You might need to say it again tomorrow, and the day after, and the day after that; but still, for today you can say, "As for me and my household, we will serve the LORD!"

53. Dooby Dooby Doo

By Kim Longden

"Look mom!" my three-year-old said proudly, "I'm decorating!" I looked up from my computer to see that I had been so engrossed in typing, I hadn't noticed my daughter, less than two feet away, covering my printer with stickers.

Experiencing the nightmare of removing stubborn stickers from all kinds of things has made me institute a pretty strict *"stickers only go on paper"* rule around here, so my knee-jerk reaction was to chastise the little interior decorator properly. Before I said anything, though, I heard a quiet *"dooby, dooby-doo"* in the back of my mind; and I paused, smiled, and got a little teary eyed.

Back in the 1990s, Bud Ice ran these beer commercials (stay with me here) where people were terrified of a little penguin, who was wreaking all kinds of adorable havoc. In the overly-dramatic commercial scenes, the penguin would suddenly appear, saying, *"dooby, dooby-doo"* in a sing-songy voice to the tune of "Strangers in the Night."

This inevitably caused over-the-top fear and panic for the people in the commercials. I remember, my family thought these commercials were so funny at the time! (I found them online recently, and could only shake my head at the cheesiness—ha-ha!)

Back in the 90s, though, I thought it would be great fun to take tiny penguin stickers and put them in random places throughout my childhood home. Then, when someone happened upon one of the little penguins, I'd creepily call out, "Dooooby, dooby-doooooo" from the shadows.

I remember us all laughing about those silly penguin stickers, especially my dad. I can still hear him saying "Dooby, dooby-doo," even years later, when he would come across a forgotten penguin sticker in some random place around the house.

As a parent looking back now, I cringe a bit logistically at the thought of me putting stickers all over our home. However, if my mom and dad were annoyed by my little penguins, I don't remember it. I just remember us laughing at the shenanigans that ensued.

You see, **my parents valued people over things**; and this value was evident in the way they lived. Mom and Dad always had what they needed, but they didn't pour all their energy into material pursuits; they poured into others. Relational connections were their life investment.

And what a harvest they reaped! When my mom died a couple of years ago, I was completely amazed at the number of people who said they had heard about Christ from her! The line at my dad's visitation went through the building and out the door with people whose lives he had touched in some way, because he was the kind of person who would strike up a conversation with anyone.

My parents' earthly, material legacy was not vast, but the ripple effect of their relationships is a heavenly legacy that will continue for generations. They truly invested in the things that "moth and rust cannot destroy," and I am eternally blessed to be a part of that legacy.

Looking at my sticker-covered printer brought tears to my eyes as I remembered my parents and how they lived out their priorities and values. This brief "dooby, dooby-doo" pause made me look at my daughter's "decorating" differently.

We had just put up our Christmas tree, and I knew my three-year-old was riding out the excitement over how fun it was to decorate when she took up the task of making my printer look festive. Instead of chastising, I gave her a hug and told her how beautiful it looked.

Does this mean I'll give up my *stickers only go on paper* rule?

No; I still have my sanity to consider.

But I think I will pause more often to consider whether some "thing" is really a big deal, or possibly an opportunity for a "dooby, dooby-doo" connection moment.

People over things.

Thanks, Mom and Dad

54. The Miracle of the Floating Axhead

By Justin Rossow

The company of the prophets said to Elisha, "Look, the place where we meet with you is too small for us. Let us go to the Jordan, where each of us can get a pole; and let us build a place there for us to live." And he said, "Go."

Then one of them said, "Won't you please come with your servants?" "I will," Elisha replied. And he went with them.

They went to the Jordan and began to cut down trees. As one of them was cutting down a tree, the iron axhead fell into the water. "Oh, my lord," he cried out, "it was borrowed!"

The man of God asked, "Where did it fall?" When he showed him the place, Elisha cut a stick and threw it there, and made the iron float. "Lift it out," he said. Then the man reached out his hand and took it.

2 Kings 6:1-7 (NIV)

It sounds like something from *The National Enquirer*, not the Bible! At first blush, this Miracle of the Floating Axhead seems to behave less like a miracle and more like a fairy tale, and a bad one at that! Take the borrowed axhead and add a prince or a pot of gold and then you could be on to something. But throwing a stick onto a river lacks the Copperfield heroics our Hollywood mindset expects.

We tend to think of supernatural wonders as being reserved for special people and special occasions. Miracles have something of fairy dust and leprechauns about them in our modern mind. What's so spectacular about gardening equipment? This miracle seems so mundane, so droll, so blue collar.

And yet ... and yet, it made the cut. It survived the final draft. The Miracle of the Floating Axhead has been preserved across centuries because God would speak to us precisely here: precisely in this nine-to-five, rank and file, working stiff miracle.

As we take a closer look at this bizarre miracle, we find it isn't all that out of place. If you've read 2 Kings recently (and come on, who has...) then you know this section of the Bible is full of miracles.

In the opening verses of chapter four, Elisha multiplies cooking oil for a widow of the company of prophets. Then he brings a dead boy back to life by stretching out on top of him. Another time, when the company of prophets were over for a potluck, they discover poison gourds had been added to the stew. Elisha adds some flour and miraculously the "death in the pot" is cured. Chapter four closes with the miraculous feeding of a hundred men while chapter five gives the detailed account of the healing of a prominent foreign army officer: Naaman's leprosy is cured when he obeys Elisha's command and bathes seven times in the Jordan River.

For two whole chapters we have seen time and time again how God intervenes miraculously to protect or help God's own special people. And then we get to the beginning of chapter six—The Miracle of the Floating Axhead—and we can expect more of the same.

Suddenly it doesn't seem so odd that God would care about the loss of an axhead. The man was a part of the company of prophets, sort of like a vicar or a pastor on internship. Besides, when all your friends and relatives are still in the Bronze Age, an iron axhead is certainly valuable. And don't forget, the thing was borrowed; the prophet in training would owe someone big bucks if he lost it, on top of the student loans he was already paying. This guy was in deep trouble! But he knew where to turn for help. Perhaps it's not so strange that the man of God would take an interest in his predicament.

No more strange, then, is the mundane methodology of this mid-sized miracle; a simple stick thrown in the water is no less dramatic than any of the miracles preceding it. A jar of oil for a widow, a handful of flour for the stew, a hug for a dead boy, some bread for a hundred hungry, some water for a leper—all of these are common, everyday, ordinary means.

No glitz. No glitter. No dry ice machine or pulsing spotlights. Just God acting for ordinary people, letting them know again and again Who is in charge, Who has control, Who is able to do miraculous things—letting these people know again and again how much God cares for them.

This odd miracle, then, doesn't seem so odd after all. In fact, it's just like our God to do something like that. It's just like our God to break into the lives of ordinary people to bless and deliver and save. That's kind of how our God works.

Just think of Jesus—his whole life is God breaking into our existence in order to save. When, like Elisha, Jesus heals the sick or raises the dead, his message is the same: God is at work for these ordinary people.

Elisha shows God at work, but Jesus does Elisha one better. Jesus raises the dead without full-body calisthenics; he simply speaks or takes a little hand in his. Jesus heals lepers by a word, not a river. Jesus feeds *five thousand* men. Jesus shows by his miracles that he is like the prophets of old, only better. Jesus is the fulfillment of the prophets' promise. Jesus is the feast of God acting for ordinary people; Elisha was part of the appetizer.

But the two belong to the same meal: the same God is at work. The same procedure is often followed. The same message is proclaimed.

If you look closely, the methods Jesus uses to show God's power breaking into the daily grind of human busyness seem strangely ordinary; strangely familiar, in fact. A jar of water, a handful of mud, a word, some bread, some wine—all of these common, ordinary means.

No glitz. No glitter. No dry ice machine or pulsing spotlights. Just God acting for ordinary people, letting them know again and again Who is in charge—letting these people know again and again how much God cares for them.

If you look closely around the sanctuary on any given Sunday morning or Wednesday night, you'll see that our God is still at it—Jesus is still acting for ordinary people to let them know how much he cares.

If you look around the sanctuary, you will see some rather ordinary things: a handful of water, a word, some bread, some wine. Through these ordinary means, Jesus is still working miracles in the ordinary, busy lives of his people. Here Jesus comes and gives us himself and makes us his own. Here we "touch and handle things unseen."

As you take the wafer in your mouth, as you touch the chalice to your lips, Jesus is there for you. God is miraculously touching your life. You are forgiven. I can't promise you every sinking axhead will float again, but your debt has been paid; your sin is forgiven. God is acting for ordinary people—what a miracle!

And, wonder of wonders, it doesn't stop there. Jesus outdid Elisha, but he's not done yet. Jesus is even going to outdo himself. No matter how wonderful the Lord's Supper is—and it is a miracle! Here Christ Himself is present for us. Here our sins are forgiven. Here we are shaped into the body of Christ—no matter how tightly our faith grasps this foretaste of the feast to come, it is only a *foretaste* of **the feast to come.**

A time is coming soon when we will no longer walk by faith, but by sight. A time is coming soon when Christ will cease to act in humble, hidden means and every knee shall bow and every tongue confess that Jesus is Lord.

A time is coming soon when—like the widow's son—all the dead will be raised, when—like Naaman's leprosy—all illness will be healed, when—like those who walked and ate with Jesus of Nazareth—you will see God in your own flesh. No one will miss the Son of God when he comes in blazing glory and terrible judgment.

For you, it will be a day of victory. All because here and now, God is acting for ordinary people. Jesus is forgiving their sins and making them his own. He is showing them all—Jesus is showing you—how much he cares.

Author's Note: I originally wrote this sermon for a Hom 2 (basic preaching) class at the Seminary being taught by my great uncle "Rev" Rossow. I was reminded of it recently when I mistakenly listed 2 Kings 6 (the floating axhead) as one of our weekly readings instead of 2 Kings 5 (the story of Naaman). Today I accidentally found this same sermon buried in my computer file directory while I was looking for something completely different. It made me smile to read it again, so I thought I would share it with you.

Conclusion

I've been reading and rereading Philippians lately (on assignment from our pastor, who invited all of us to read that book together this month), and I am struck not only by the joy Paul exhibits in the midst of difficulty, but how much of that joy is tied to his relationship with the actual *people* in Philippi.

Paul remembers his friends joyfully in prayer. He celebrates with them, and longs for them. Paul is encouraged by them and wants to encourage them. Paul's joy is filled up to overflowing because of their partnership, and he wants them to know how precious they are to Jesus, and to him.

Without pushing the analogy too far, I kind of feel the same way about the authors in this Next Step anthology. They not only experimented with living out their relationship with Jesus in the normalcy of their ordinary moments and days, they took time to share the gifts they discovered along the way. I am so encouraged by their writing; I celebrate their partnership; they cause overflowing joy for me, for their readers, and for the Jesus who delights over them with singing.

I am so grateful that they help me see Jesus at work in my ordinary life. In fact, they help me trust Jesus is working in my moments and my days even when I can't see it.

As I look ahead to next year, there is so much I can't see clearly; so many unknown obstacles and detours and challenges and possibilities for me, for my family, for Next Step Press. Facing all that unknown can be a little daunting. But seeing Jesus faithfully present in the ordinary lives of these extraordinary people gives me confidence once again that Jesus is faithfully present in my ordinary life, too.

In fact, the way these authors have noticed the divine in the midst of their mundane reminds me that Jesus wraps some of his best gifts in darkness; not because he wants to hide them, but because some gifts can only be given when you don't know what happens next.

May that dependence on Jesus stay with us in all our mundane moments and ordinary days. Amen.

55. Gifts Wrapped in Darkness

By Justin Rossow

At the end of our congregational information meeting last night (on Zoom no less), one of my pastors was asked to close the gathering in prayer. "A year and a half ago, we looked at the future and saw only darkness," he prayed. "But You, God, had wrapped gifts for us in that darkness—and You blessed us as we walked into a future we couldn't see or understand."

That image of gifts wrapped in darkness really caught my attention. In this case, the darkness was specifically the uncertainty that came from COVID. You remember that uncertainty.

All of a sudden, gathering for worship stopped. The school leadership and teaching staff had to figure out how to follow CDC guidelines and offer both in-person instruction and virtual learning. Unknown budget ramifications, untenable ministry plans, and an unidentifiable path forward all meant having to slow down and take each small next step as it came. It also meant cutting other people in the congregation a lot of slack as we wrestled with what all of these decisions meant—and didn't mean—for a congregation trying to "gather, grow, and go" when *gathering* and *going* were both being reinvented on the fly!

Fast forward a year and a half, and the *growing* that took place in those challenging times is clearly evident, especially for an outsider. I'm just coming on board with this family of believers, and I have to say, I was impressed with how smoothly something as challenging as an online congregational meeting could go! Of course, we forgot to unmute once or twice; and we had the obligatory Max Headroom moment, but overall, people were friendly and gracious and patient and involved—things I haven't always experienced at in-person congregational meetings!

I don't think we could have imagined an online gathering going that well just a couple of years ago. And that's kind of the point. We have experienced and endured and embraced so many things *we couldn't have imagined* because so much of the future was unknown. Yet in the midst of the unknown, God was faithful.

The contrast between then and now was clear in the congregational meeting: back when COVID hit, our ministry options seemed narrow, our financial standing was threatened, and the school ministry was veiled in unknowable eventualities. 18 months later, the school is growing and expanding, our financial footing is more stable than it has been in years, and a sister congregation has approached us with some exciting possibilities for new ministry.

The gifts God wanted to give us were wrapped in that darkness. In some ways, the gifts required the darkness, for we never would have experienced those gifts if we had been spared the scary experience of not being able to see what was going to happen next.

But God kind of works like that. Not just during COVID, but in the ordinary life of ordinary followers, Jesus is faithfully present even when (especially when?) we don't see or understand what's going on.

Although "darkness" can stand for sin or evil or impurity or death in the Bible (in which case, "God is light, and in him is no darkness at all" 1 John 1:5), darkness can also be a place where we uniquely experience the presence of God.

In Exodus 20, the cloud of the presence of Yahweh descended on Mount Sinai, and "Moses approached *the thick darkness where God was.*" In 1 Kings 8, a similar cloud and a similar darkness descend at the dedication of the temple.

> When the priests withdrew from the Holy Place, the cloud
> filled the temple of the LORD. And the priests could not
> perform their service because of the cloud, for the glory of
> the LORD filled his temple.
>
> Then Solomon said, "The LORD has said that he would dwell
> in a dark cloud; I have indeed built a magnificent temple for
> you, a place for you to dwell forever."
>
> *1 Kings 8:10-13 (NIV)*

The Psalms use poetic language that connects the all-powerful God of the Universe with the experience of darkness.

> He made darkness his covering, his canopy around him,
> thick clouds dark with water.
>
> *Psalm 18:11 (ESV)*

> Clouds and thick darkness are all around him; righteousness
> and justice are the foundation of his throne.

Psalm 97:2 (ESV)

Generally speaking, the healing of *physical* blindness in Scripture often corresponds with overcoming *spiritual* blindness; but not always.

Saul of Tarsus is an example, not of *light*, but of *darkness* being revelatory. For all his learning, Saul was spiritually blind until the voice and the bright light on the Damascus road led him into three days of blindness. When Saul enters into darkness, it becomes for him an experience of God, a God who is too big to comprehend, but nonetheless, a God of Grace. By the time Saul (now Paul) regains his sight, he has already seen the light, because he learned to know God better in the dark. (See Acts 9.)

God, it seems, has a habit of wrapping good gifts in darkness; of making unique blessings available in, with, and under a sometimes frightening experience of the unknown.

So when you can't see the future and can't imagine what's going to happen next, trust that the God who dwells in deep darkness is with you. When your options seem limited and you can't see a way out, you are held by a God who understands what you can't and sees what you don't. You are known intimately by the God to whom the psalmist prays:

> Even the darkness will not be dark to you; the night will shine
> like the day, for darkness is as light to you.

Psalm 139:12 (NIV)

When you have to take a step forward, but your path is uncertain and your future is not clear, you *walk by faith and not by sight* (2 Corinthians 5:7). In some ways, **you have to face the dark in order to know the trust that only comes when you just can't see.**

In our lives as individuals and families, in our life together as Church, **there will always be times of uncertainty, and confusion, and darkness, and doubt.**

If my congregation does pursue planting a mission church in partnership with another congregation, there will be plenty of times when what comes next will be difficult or challenging or unknowable or ambiguous.

For all the stability my family has achieved in the last few months—new home, new school, new job—I'm sure the next question mark is just around the corner.

For all the clarity I sometimes have on how Jesus has shaped me and what Jesus has called me to do, I am always one discouraging experience away from wanting to throw in the towel because it's just too hard, and too much, and too uncertain.

But I am coming to learn more and more that the darkness of that uncertainty isn't *only* scary. (Don't get me wrong; it is scary!)

The darkness of that uncertainty is *also* exciting. **I belong to a Jesus who wraps some of his best gifts in darkness.** And I get to take one small step into the dark, with blind eyes wide open to see what Jesus is going to do next.

SDG

The Next Step Community

The Next Step Community is a group of people, like you, who need other people to help them take a next step following Jesus. You won't find any preconceived notions or quick fixes here; just real people trying to follow Jesus in real life. You are welcome to join in!

You can find us online at **community.findmynextstep.org**. We follow Jesus better when we follow Him together.

Some of the authors from *Take My Moments and My Days* can also be found in the following:

- *Jesus at the Center of My Messy Life: Tales from the Next Step Community, Year One*

- *Be Still and Notice: Tales from the Next Step Community, Year Two*

- *When from Death I'm Free: A Hymn Journal for Holy Week*

- *Ponder Anew: A Hymn Journal of Trust and Confidence*

- *Light in the Darkness: A Hymn Journal for Advent & Christmas*

Also available from Next Step Press on amazon.com:

- *Delight!: Discipleship as the Adventure of Loving and Being Loved*

- *My Next Step: A How-To Companion for People Who Want to Follow Jesus (But Sometimes Get Stuck)*

We help you take a next step.